Copyright © 2021

All Rights reserved under the international law.

First Edition

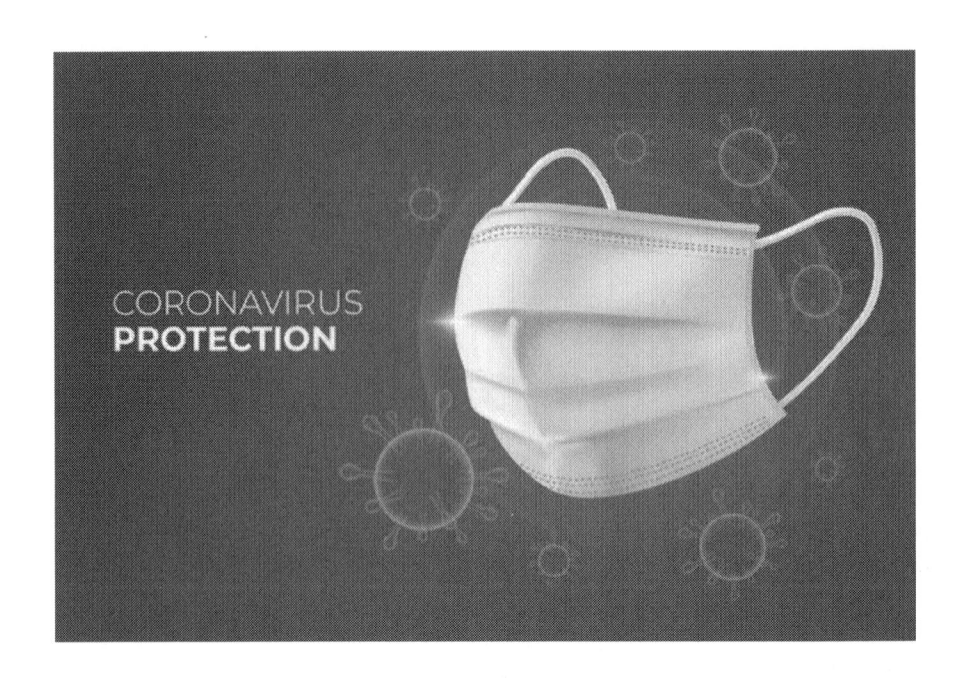

People and organizations who want to help fight the pandemic and support WHO and partners can donate through the COVID-Solidarity Response Fund.

Name:

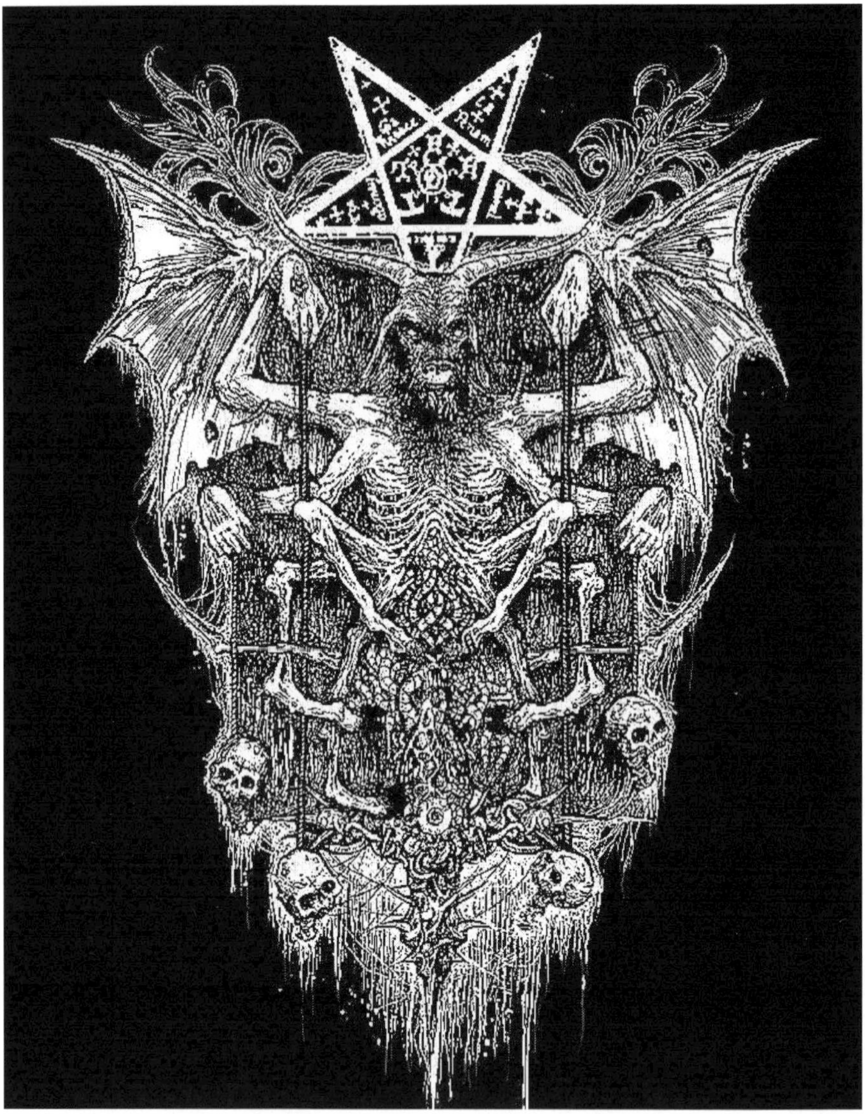

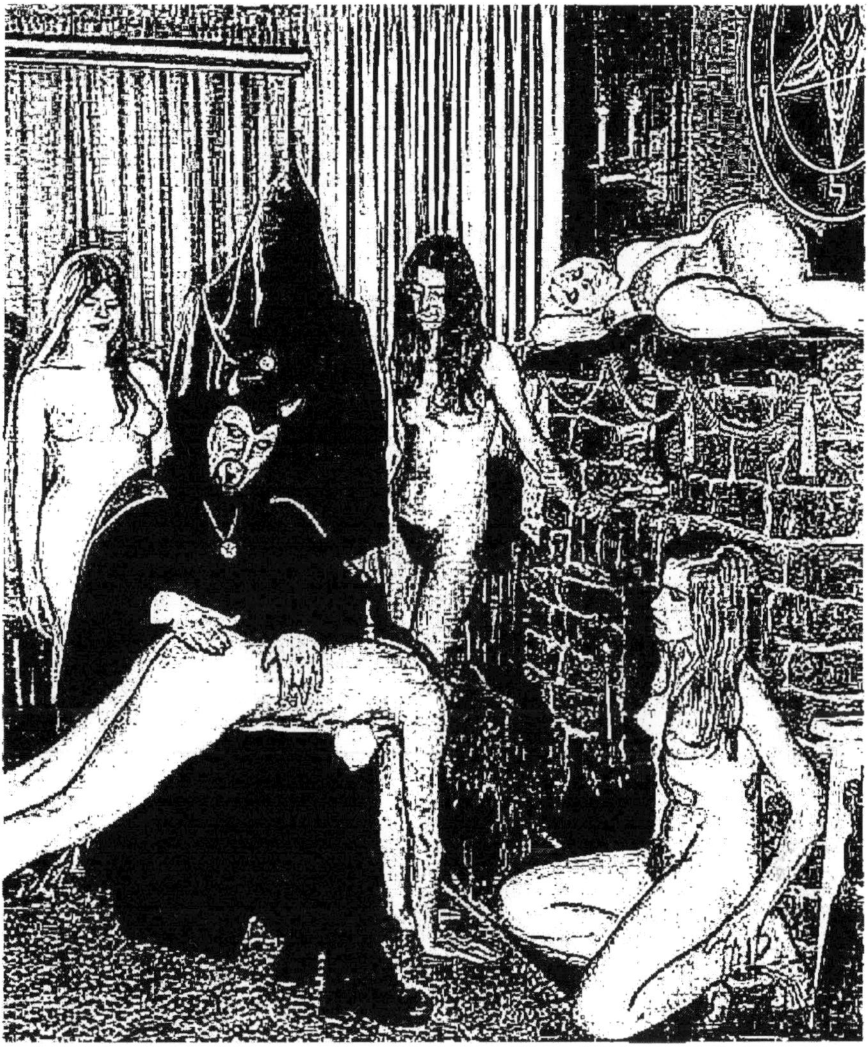

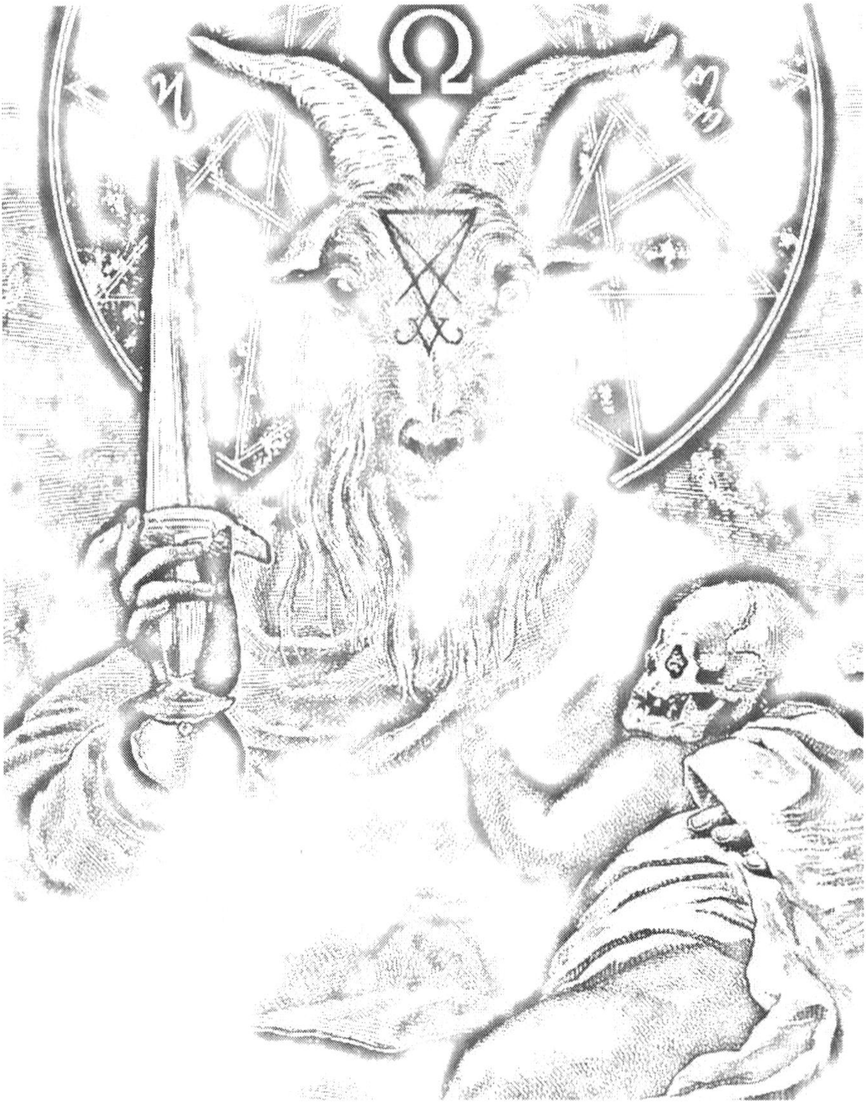

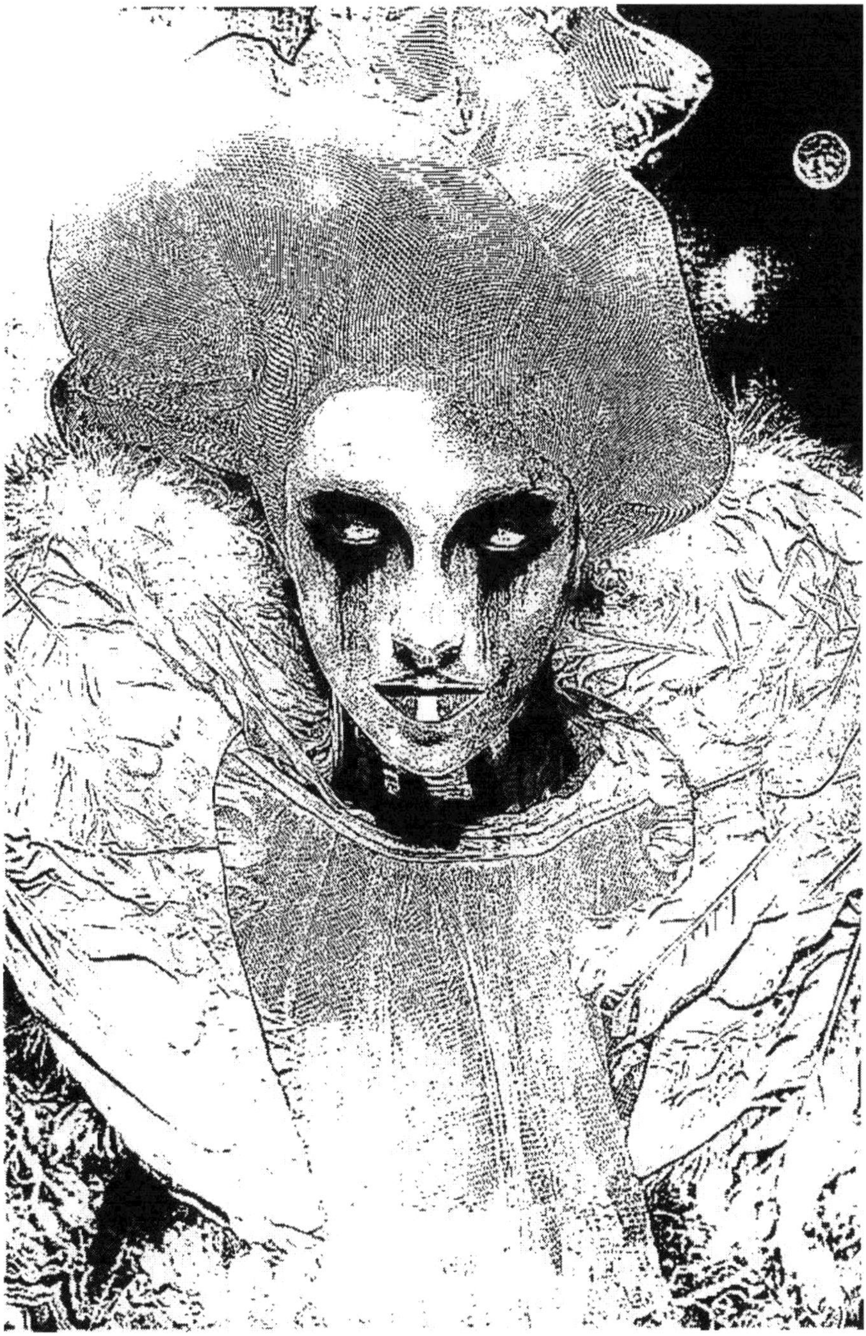

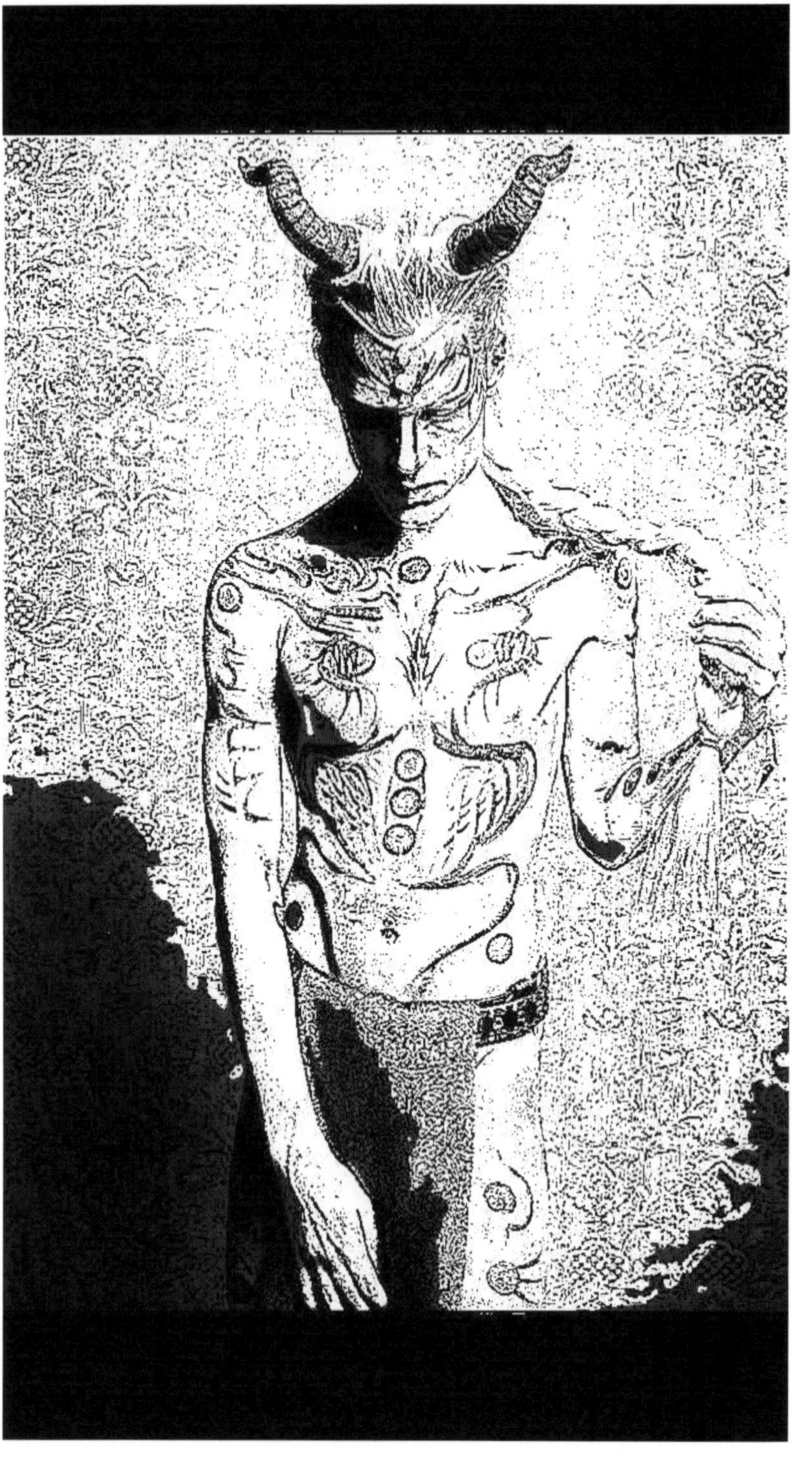

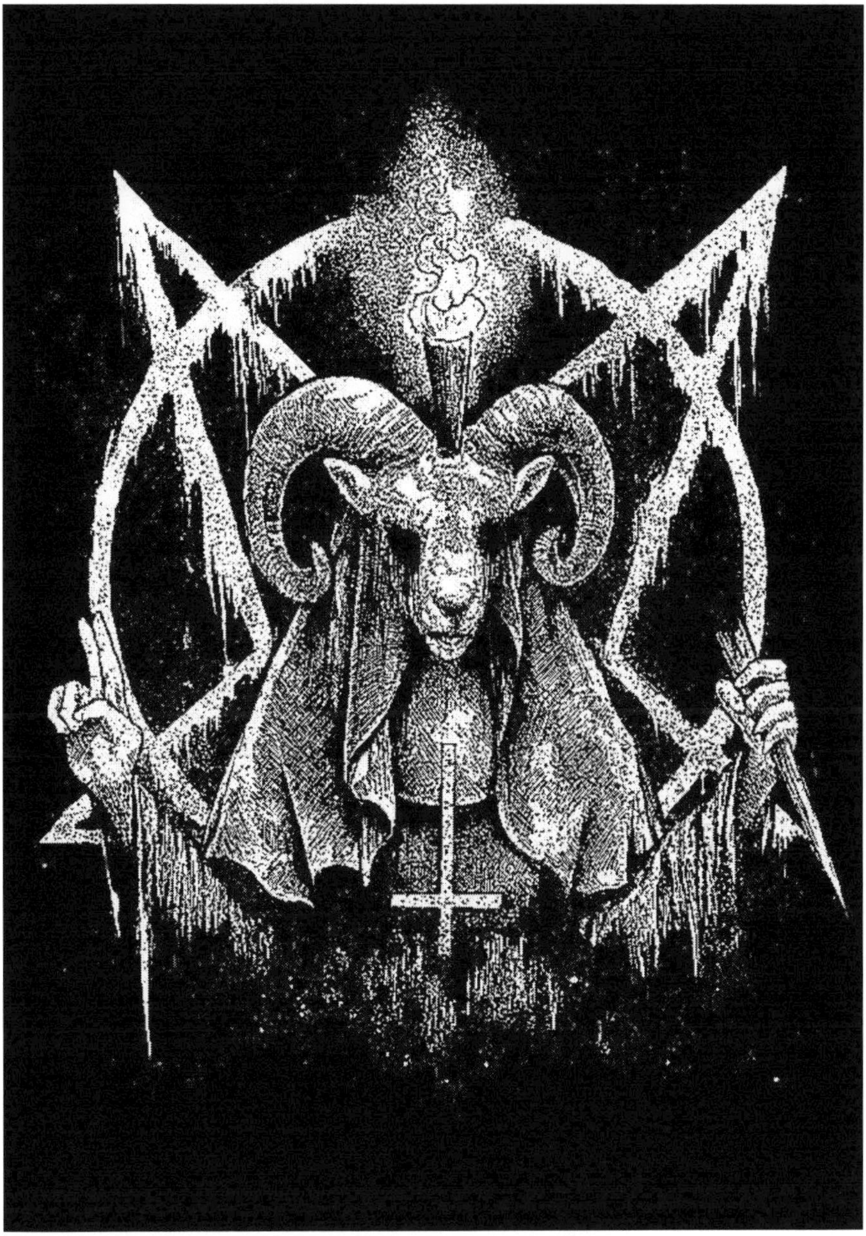

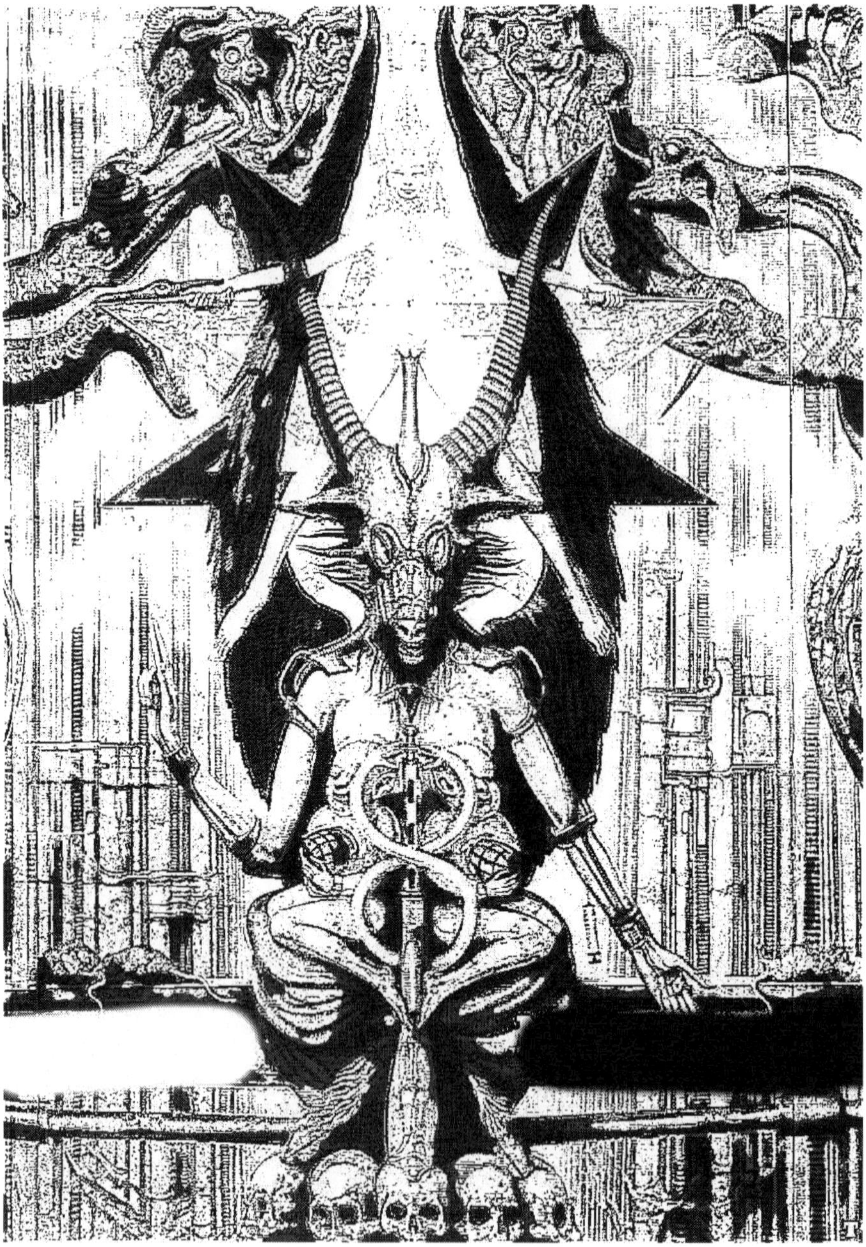

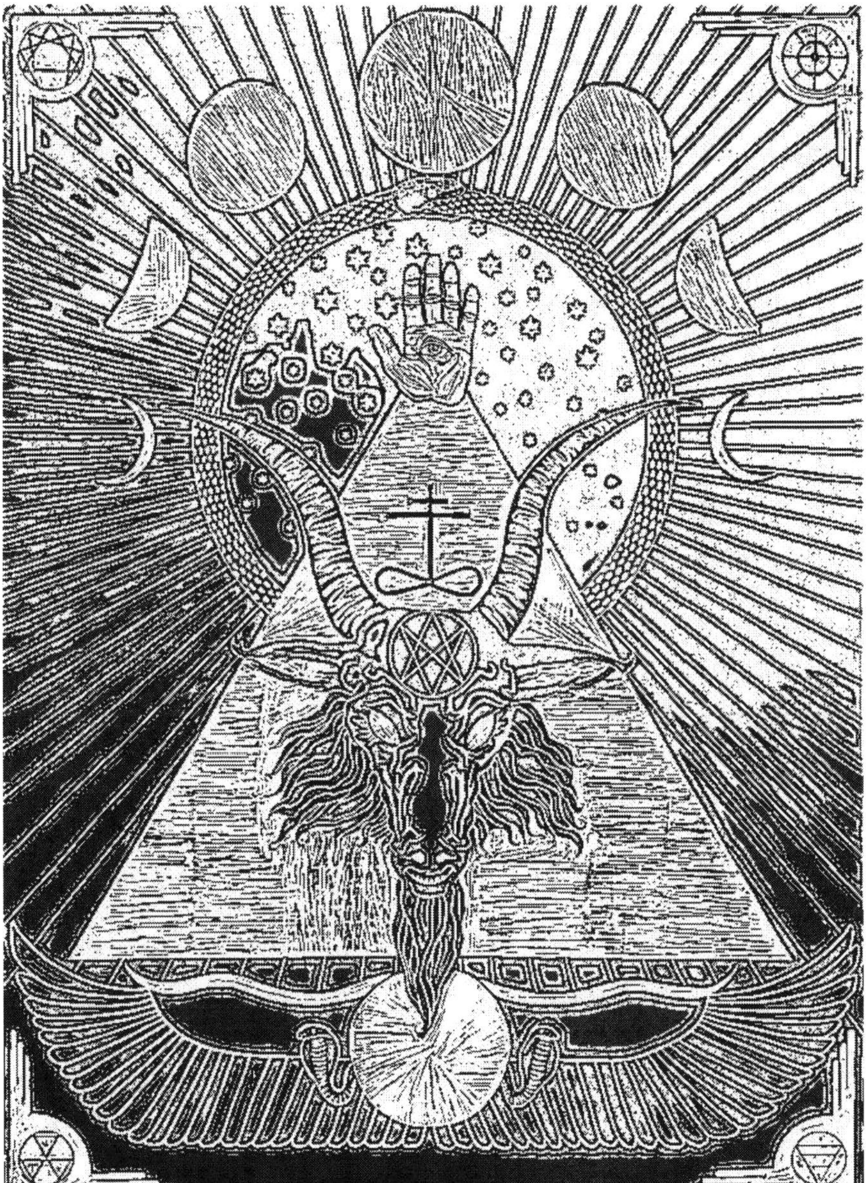

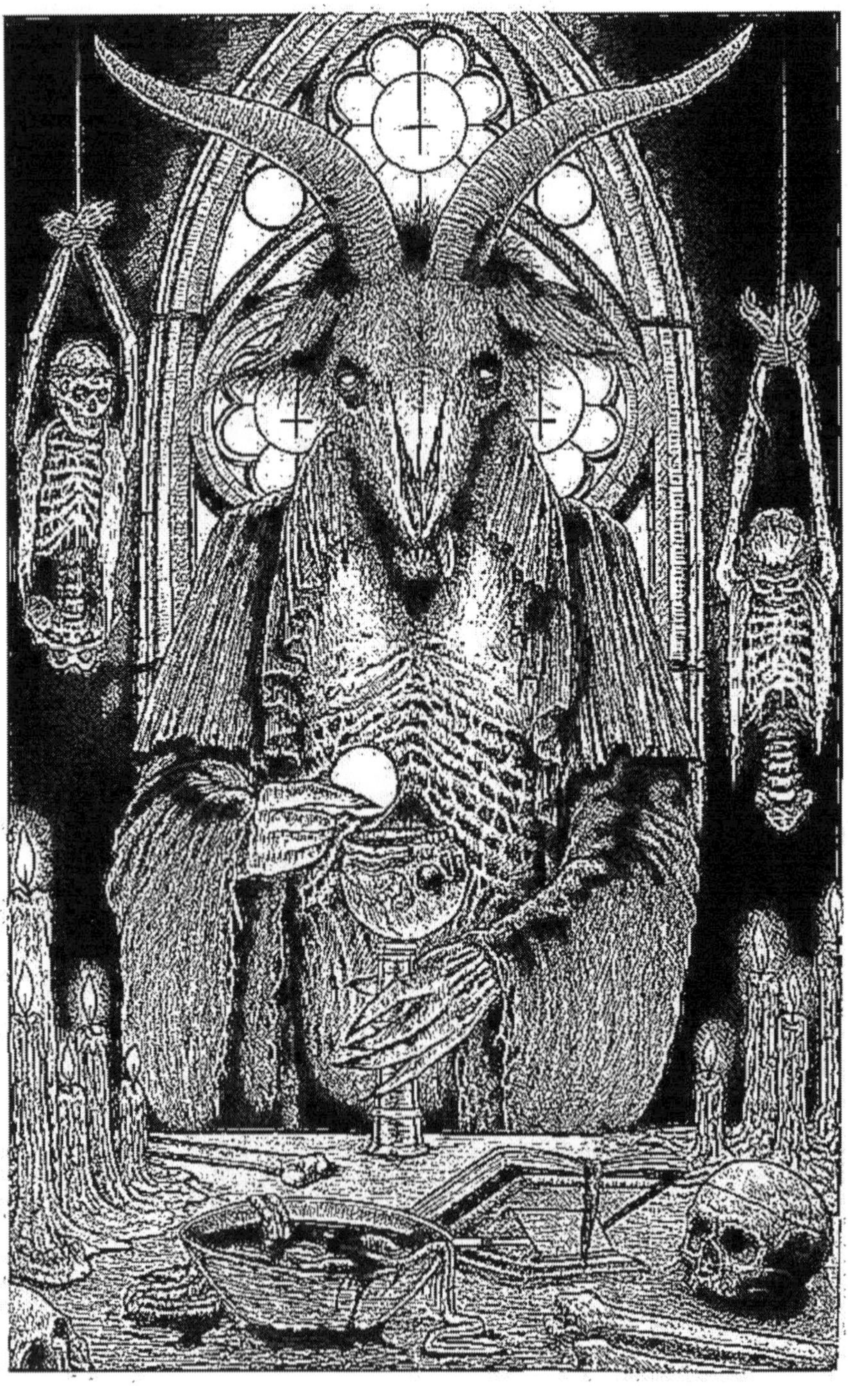

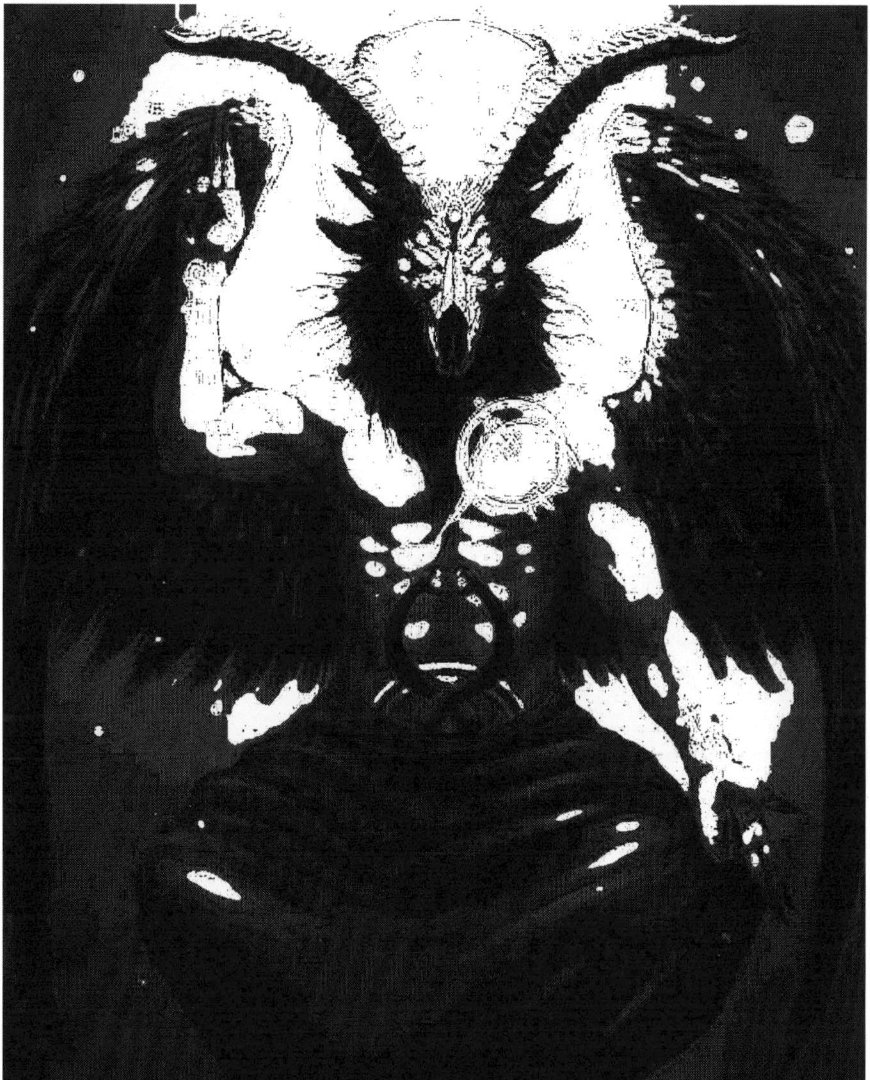

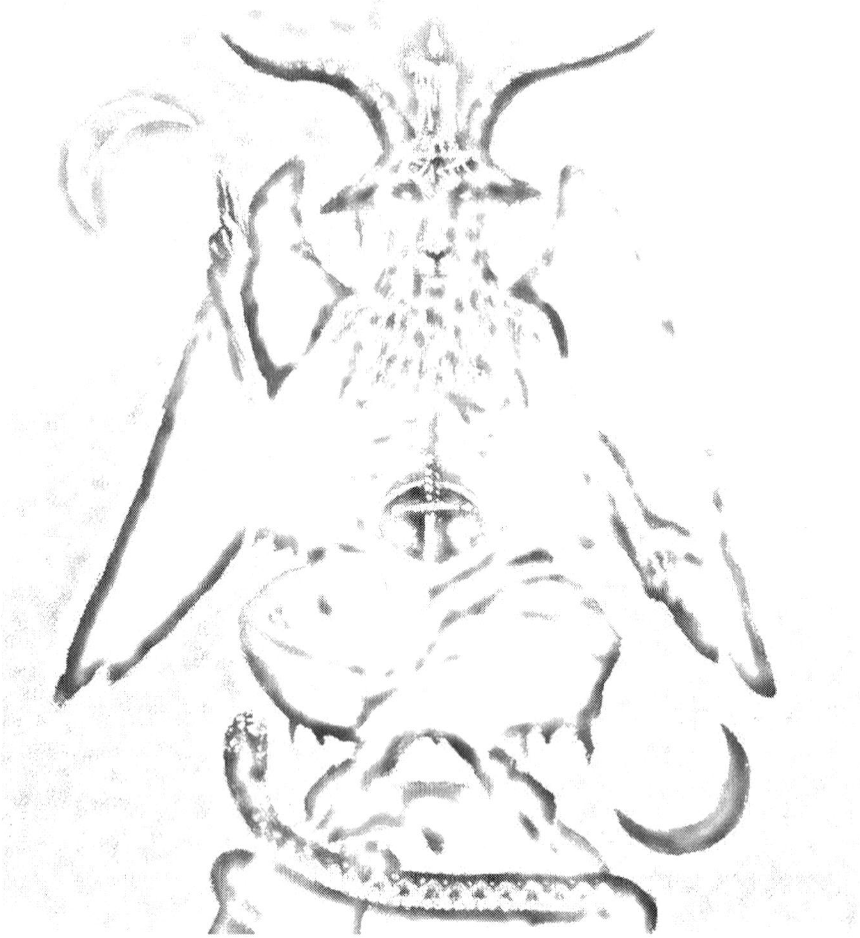

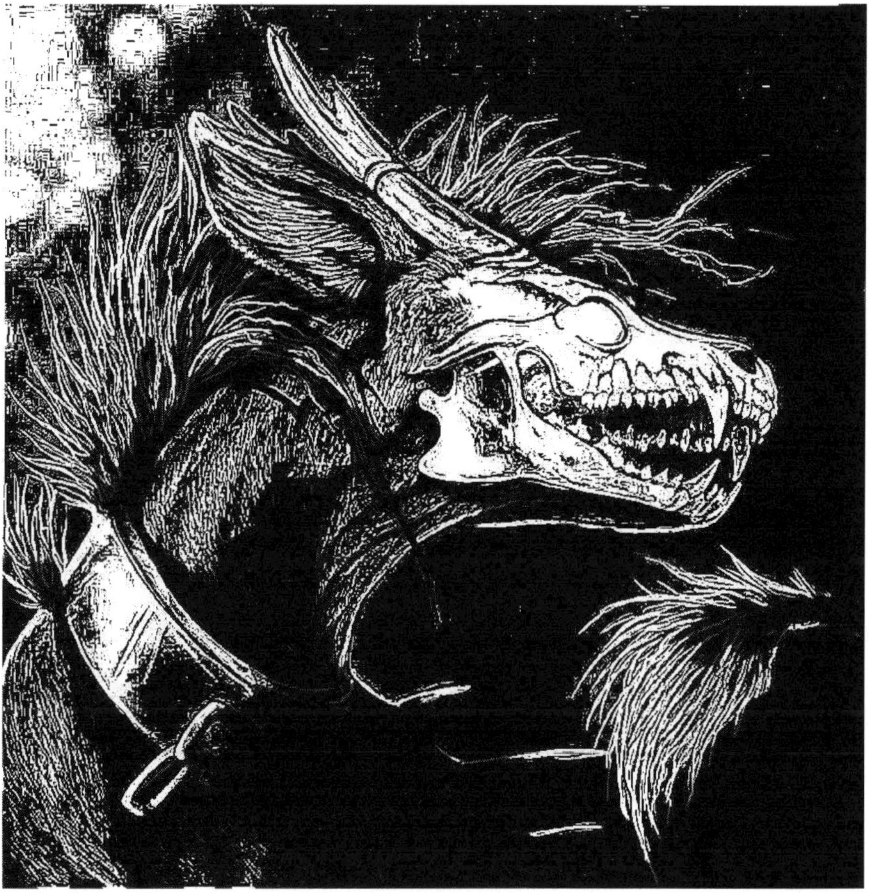

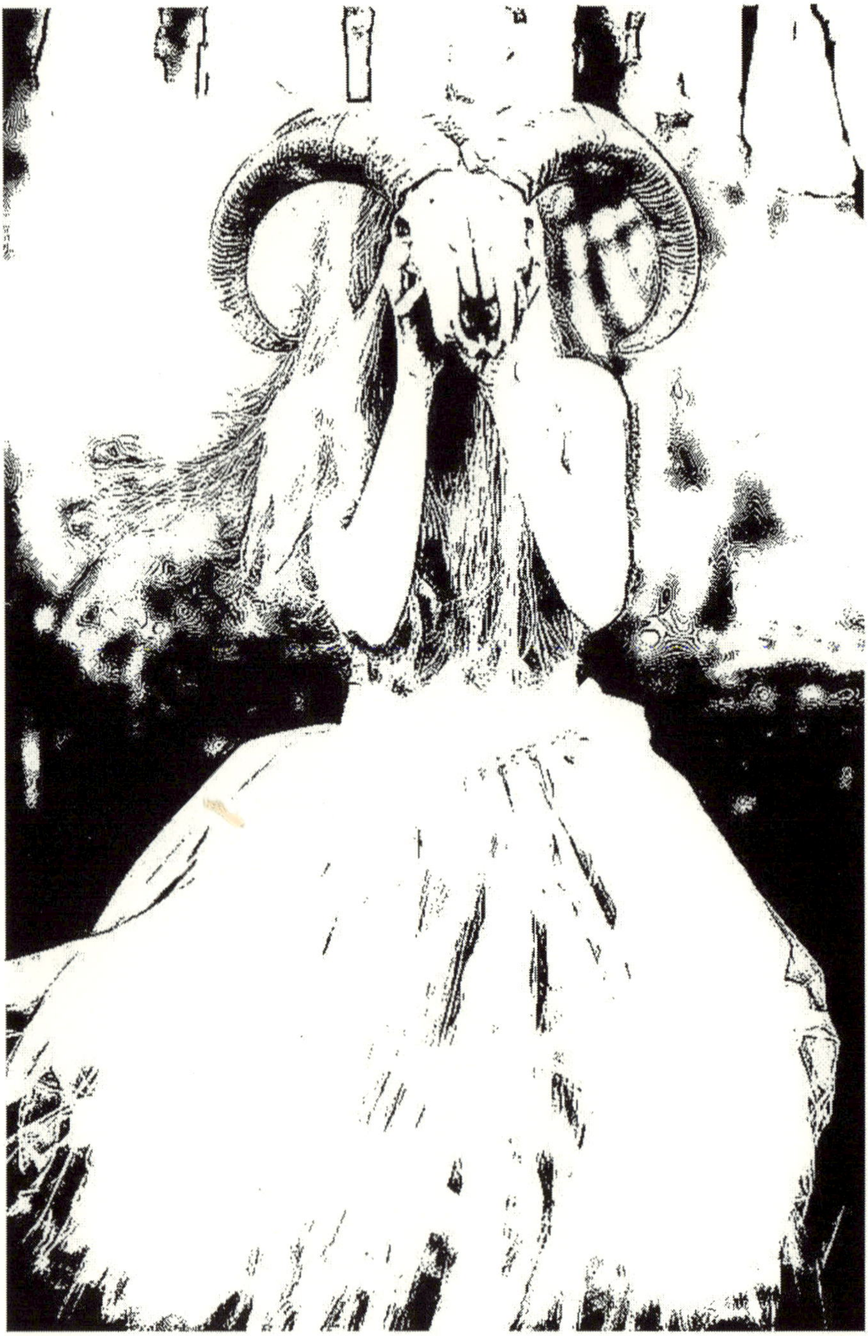

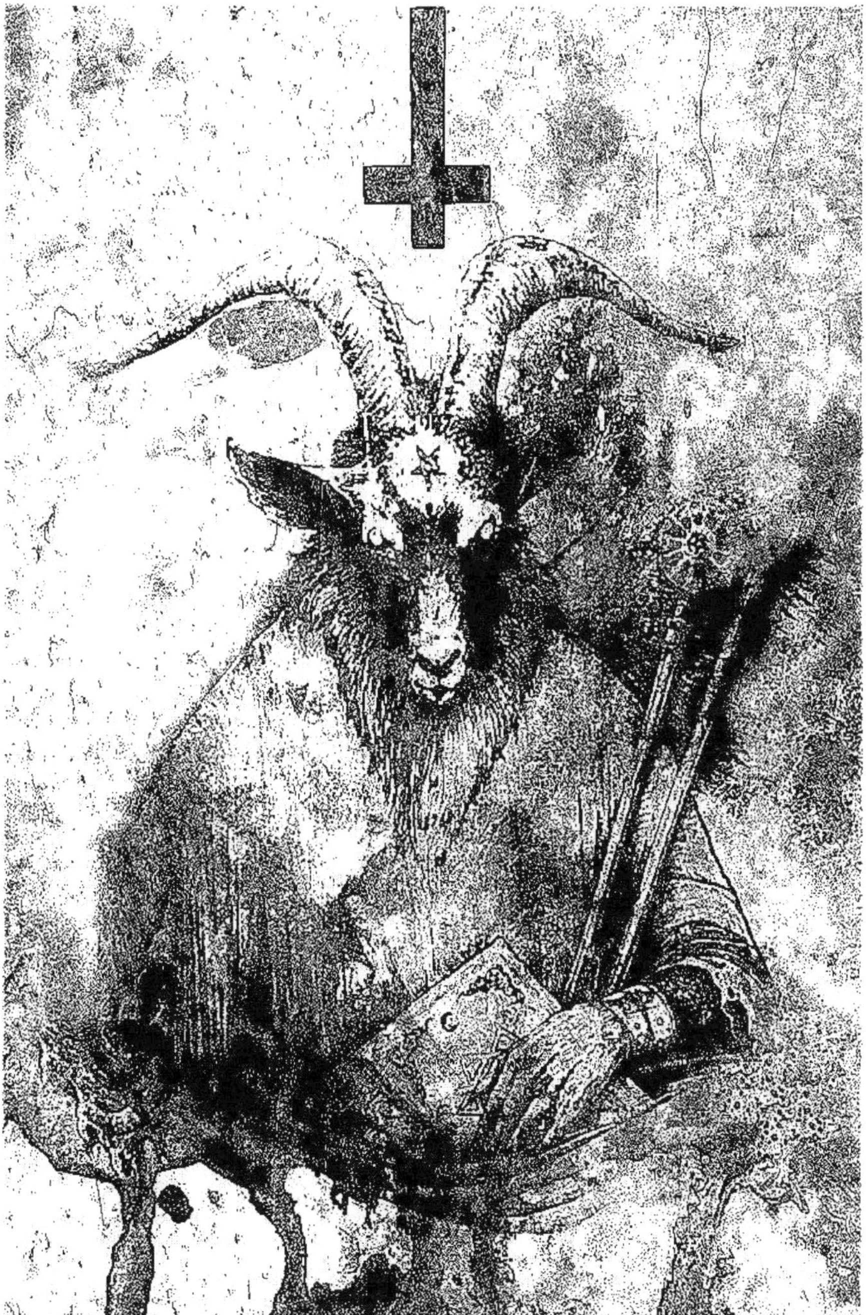

DARK VIRGIN

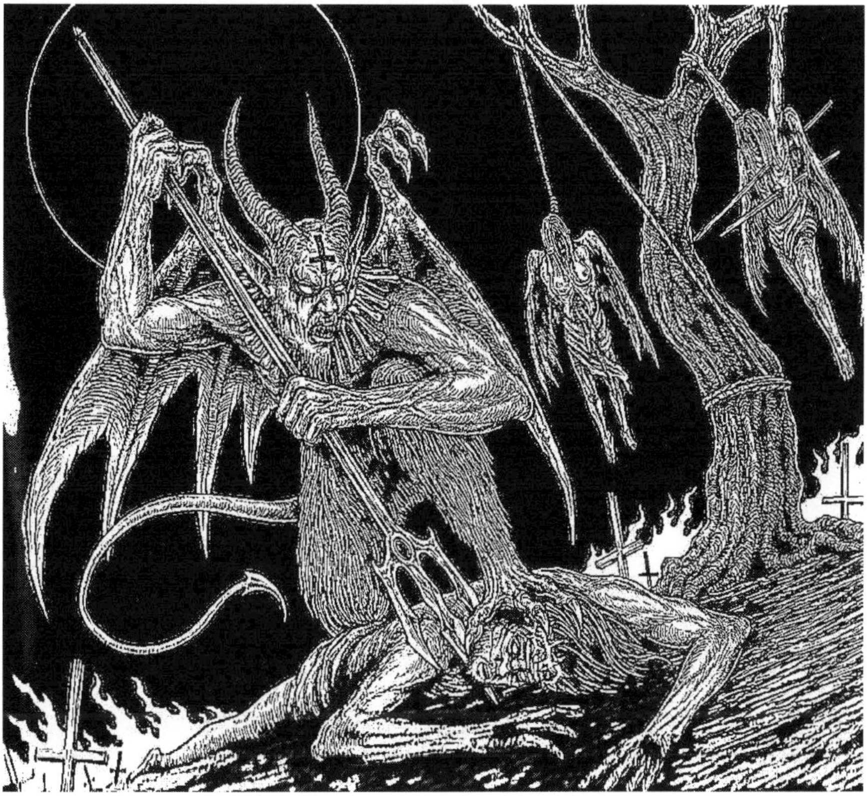

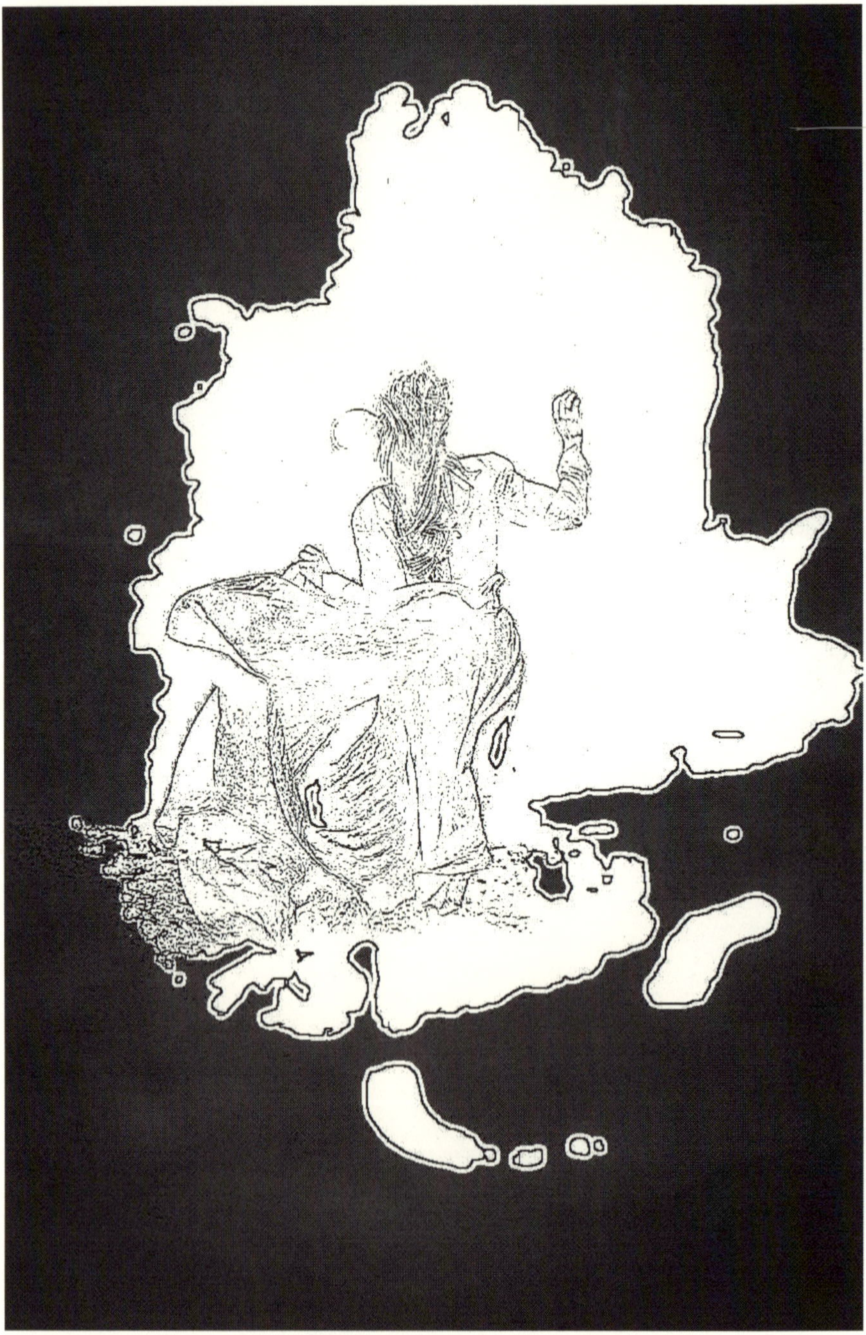

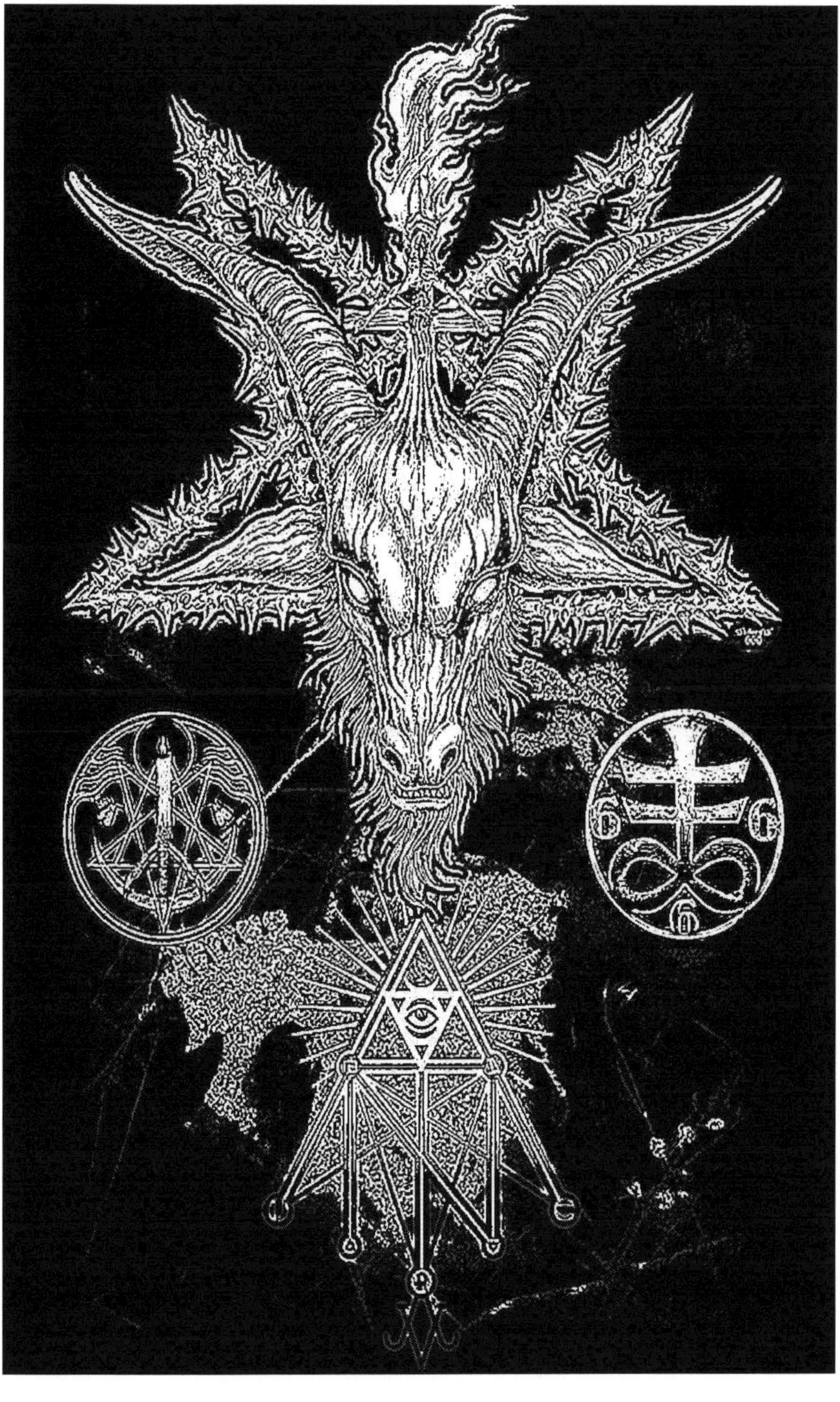

DELIVER US FROM EVIL

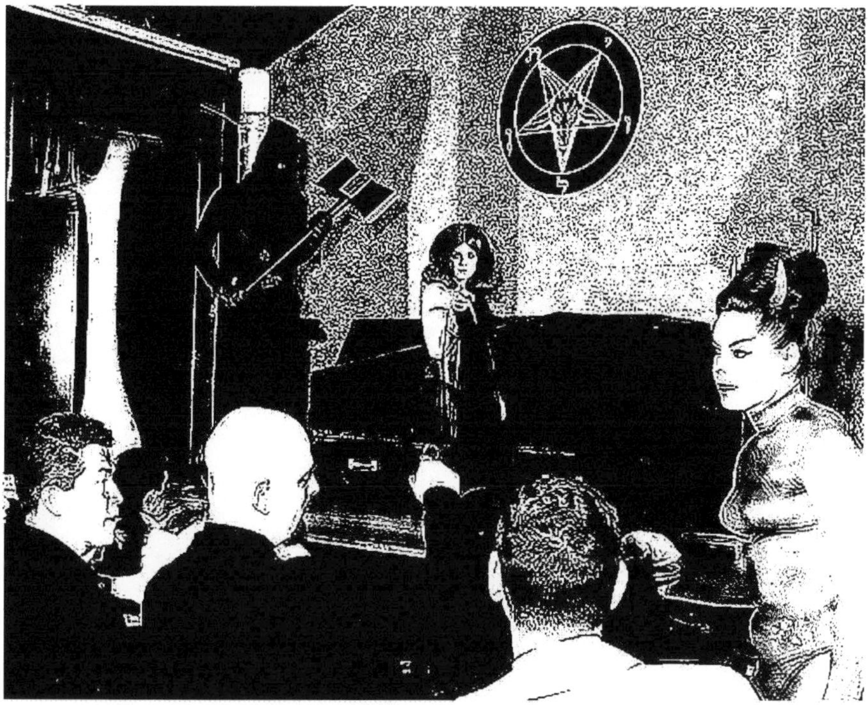

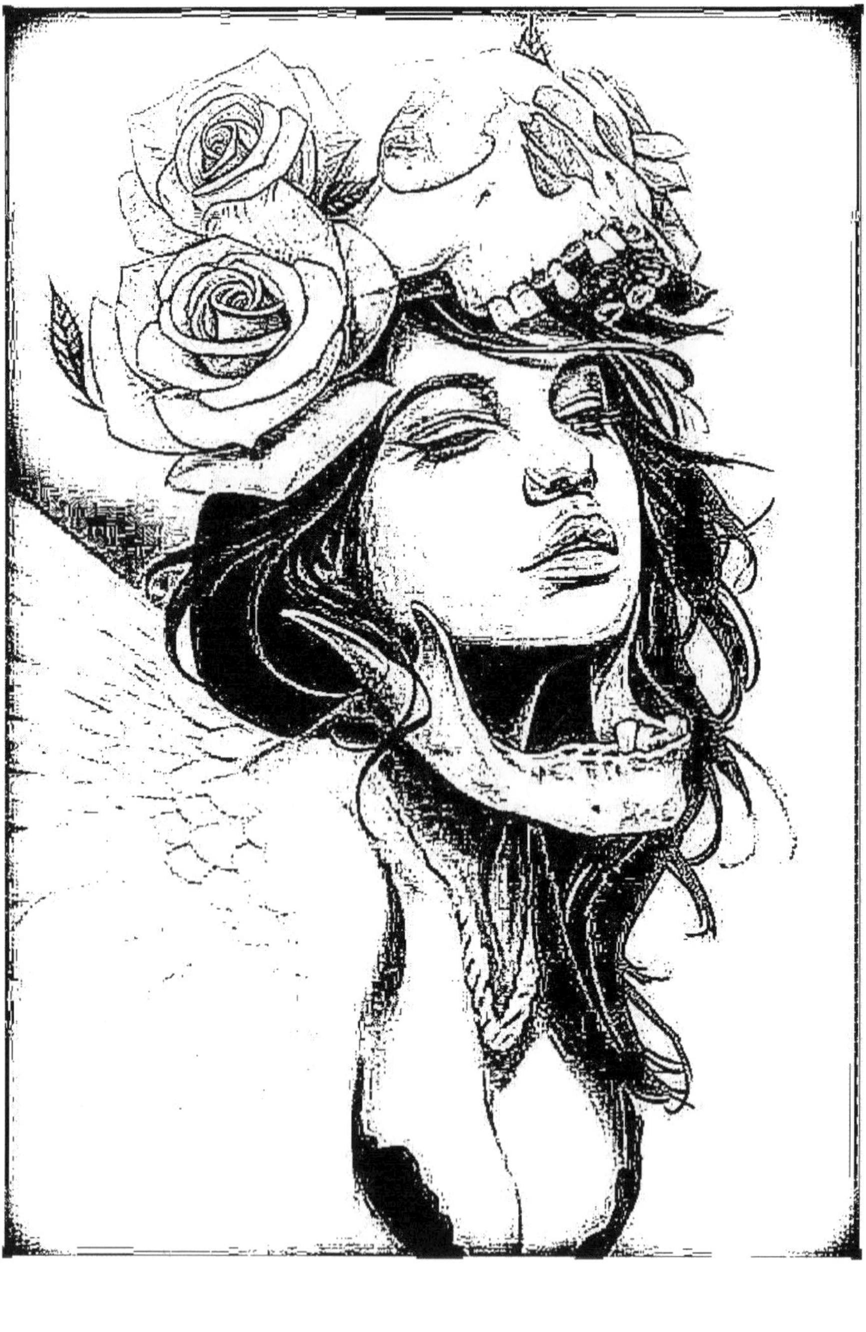

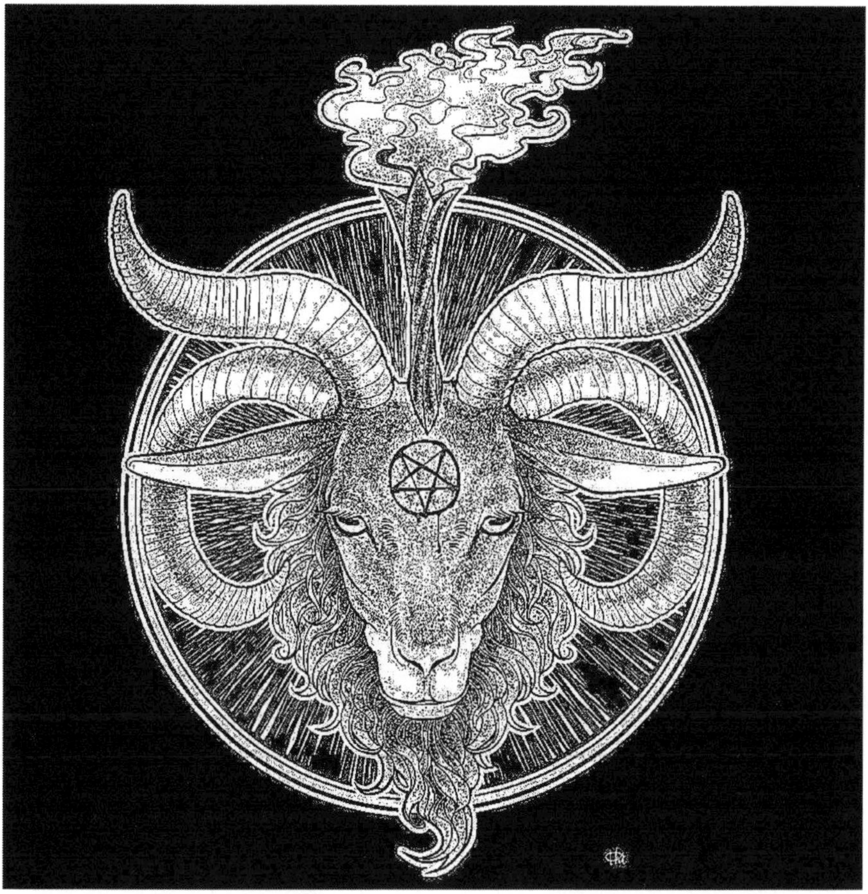

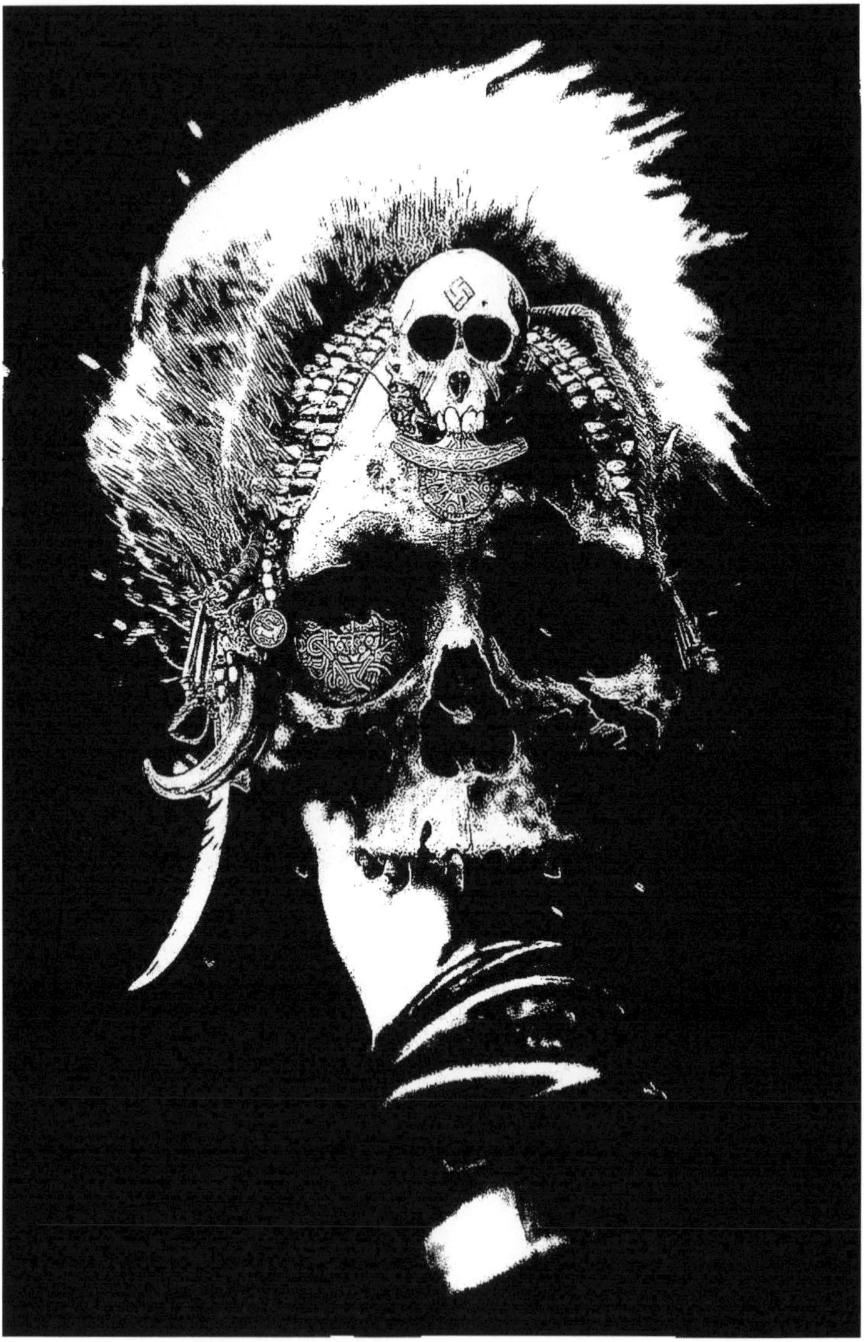

ABACROMBIE INK

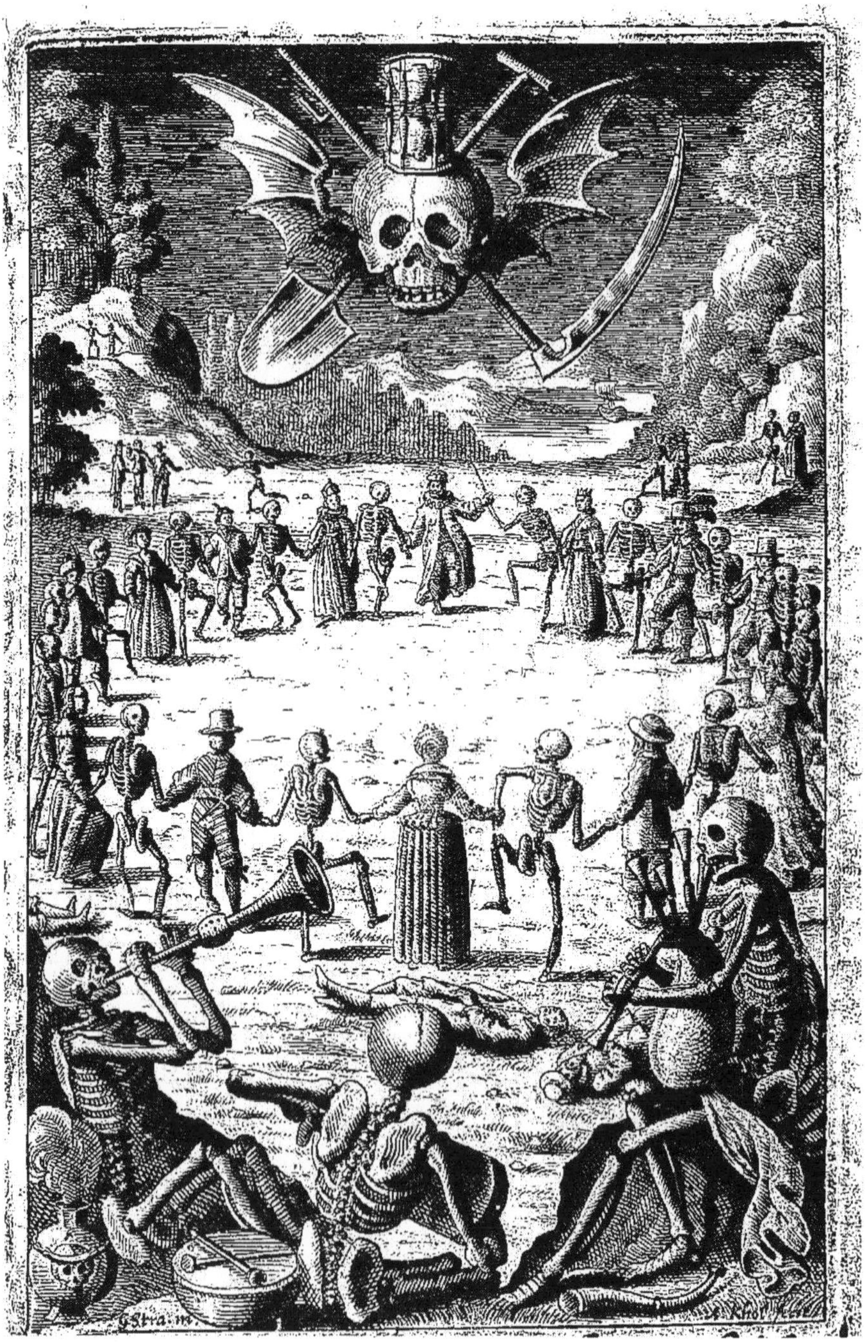

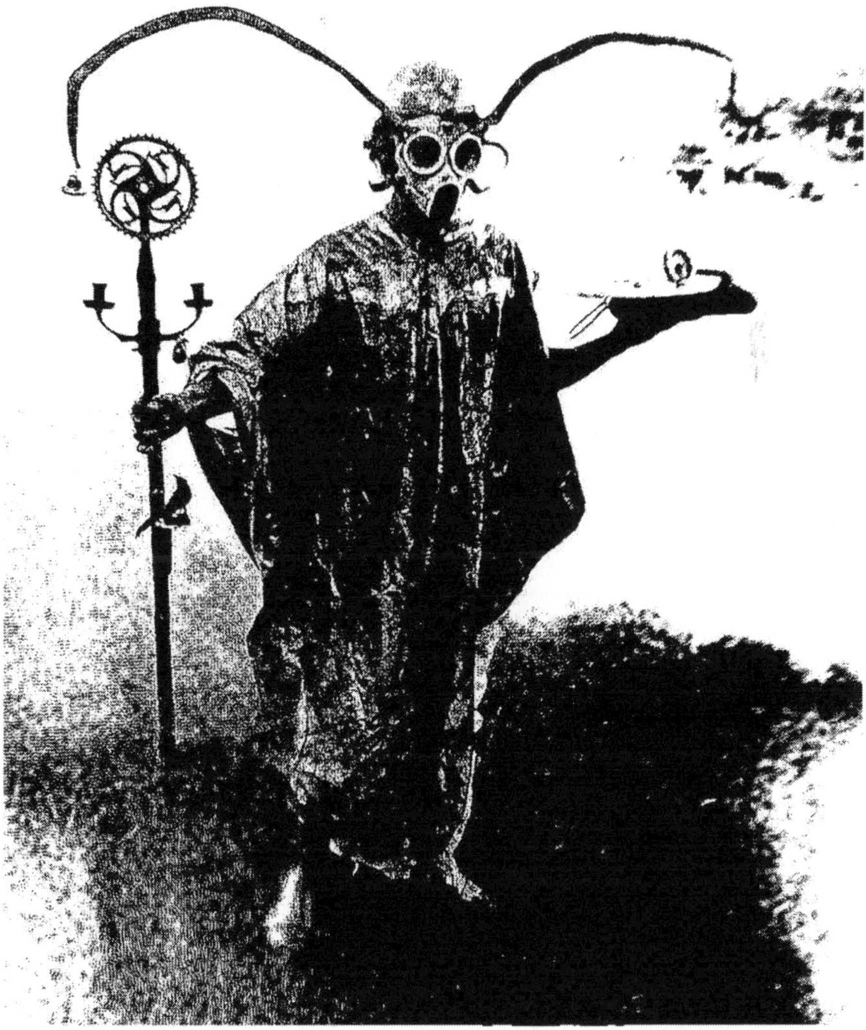

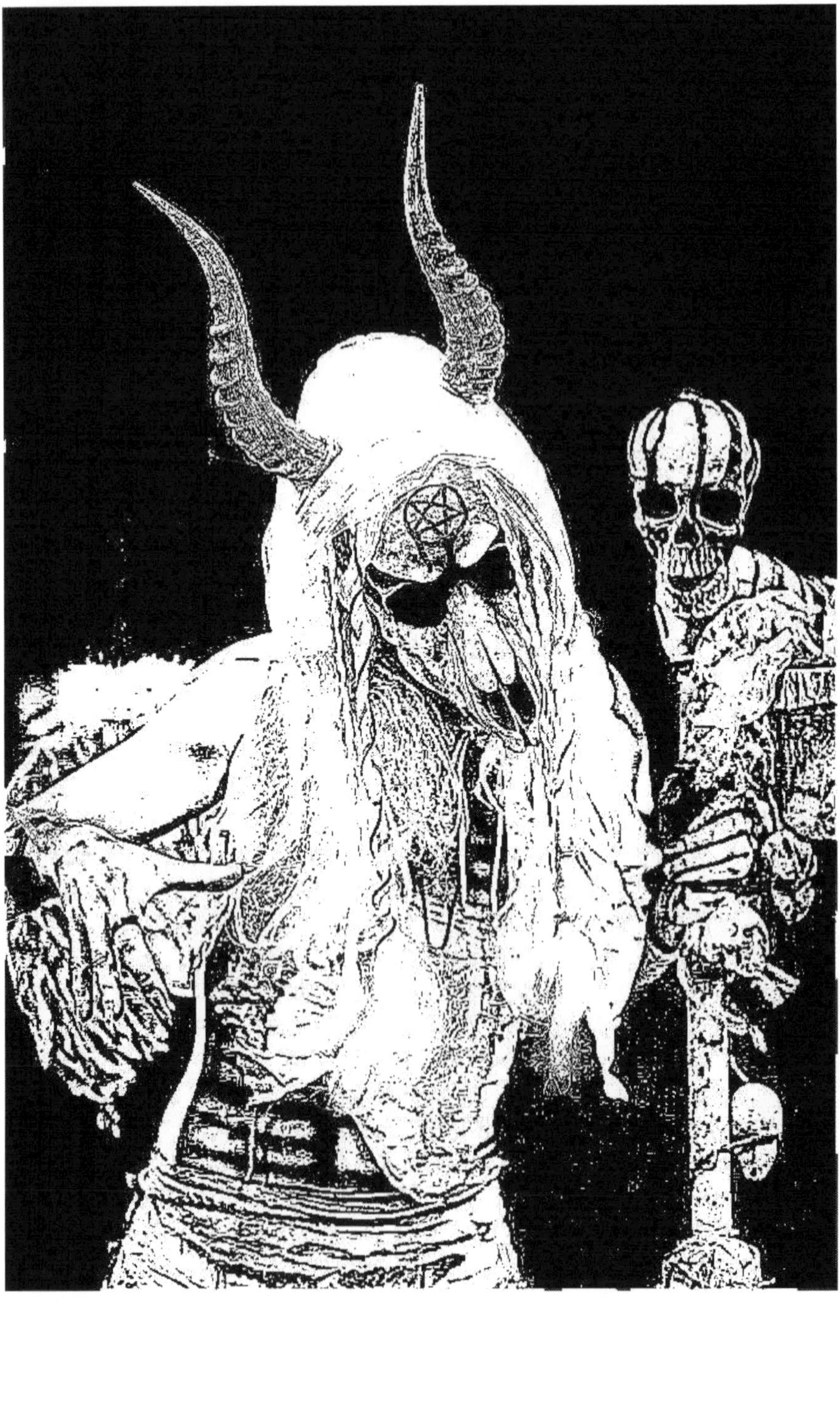

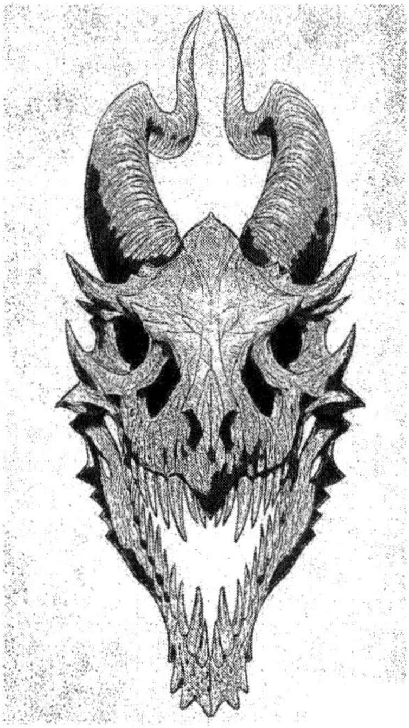

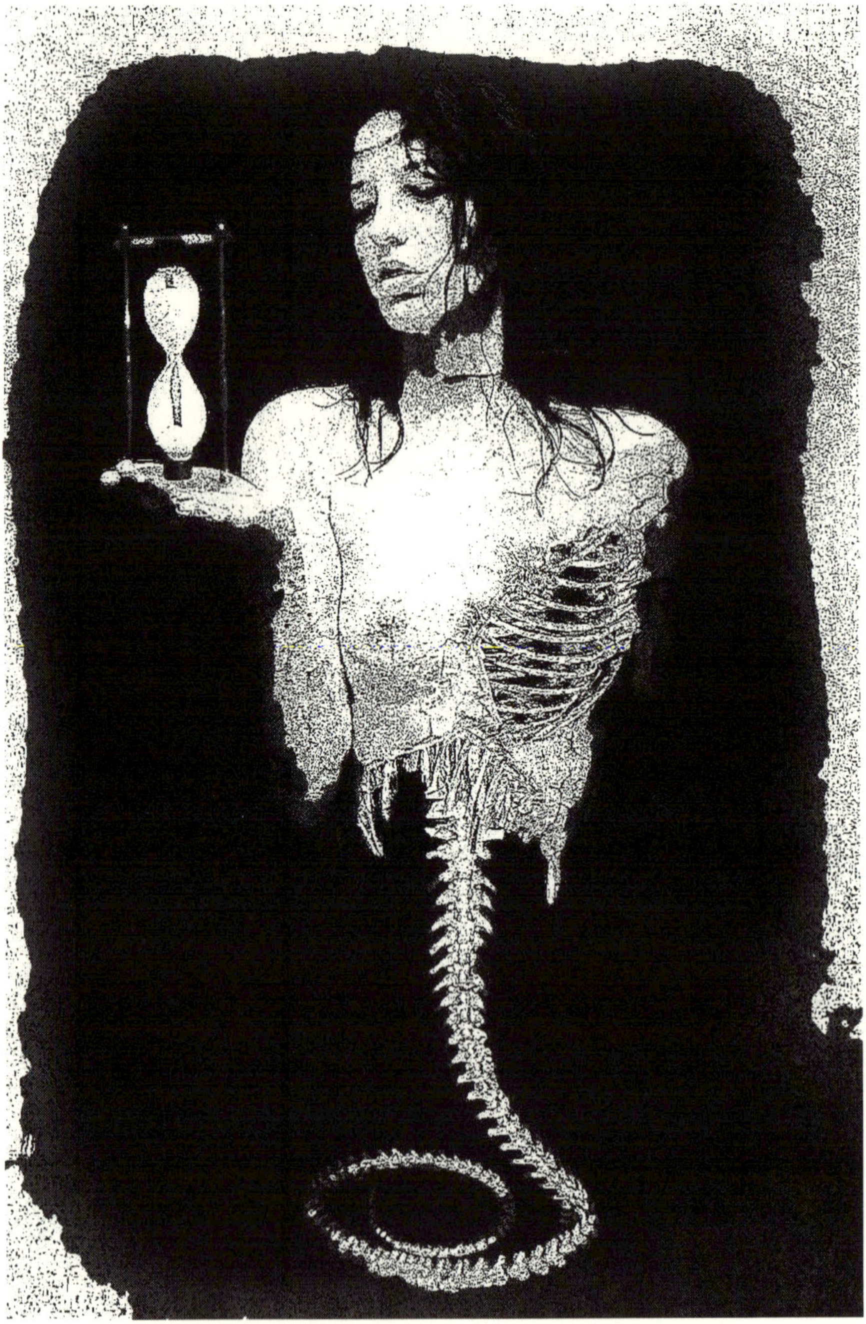

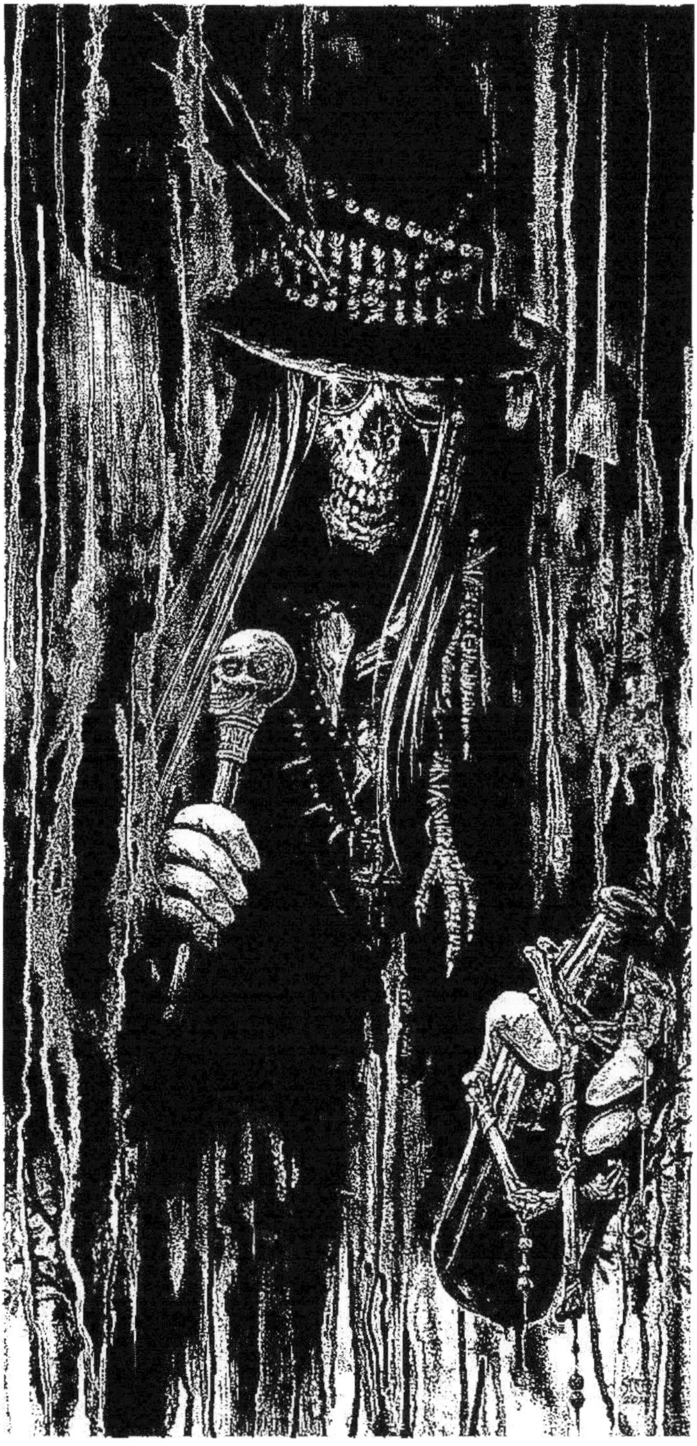

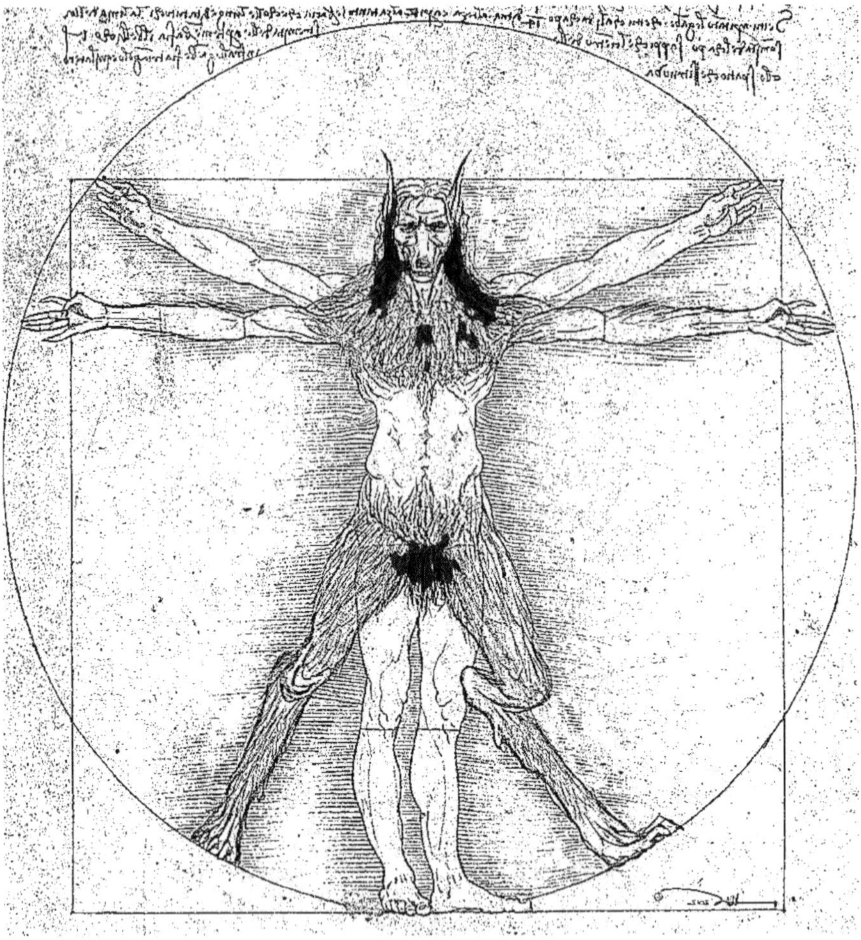

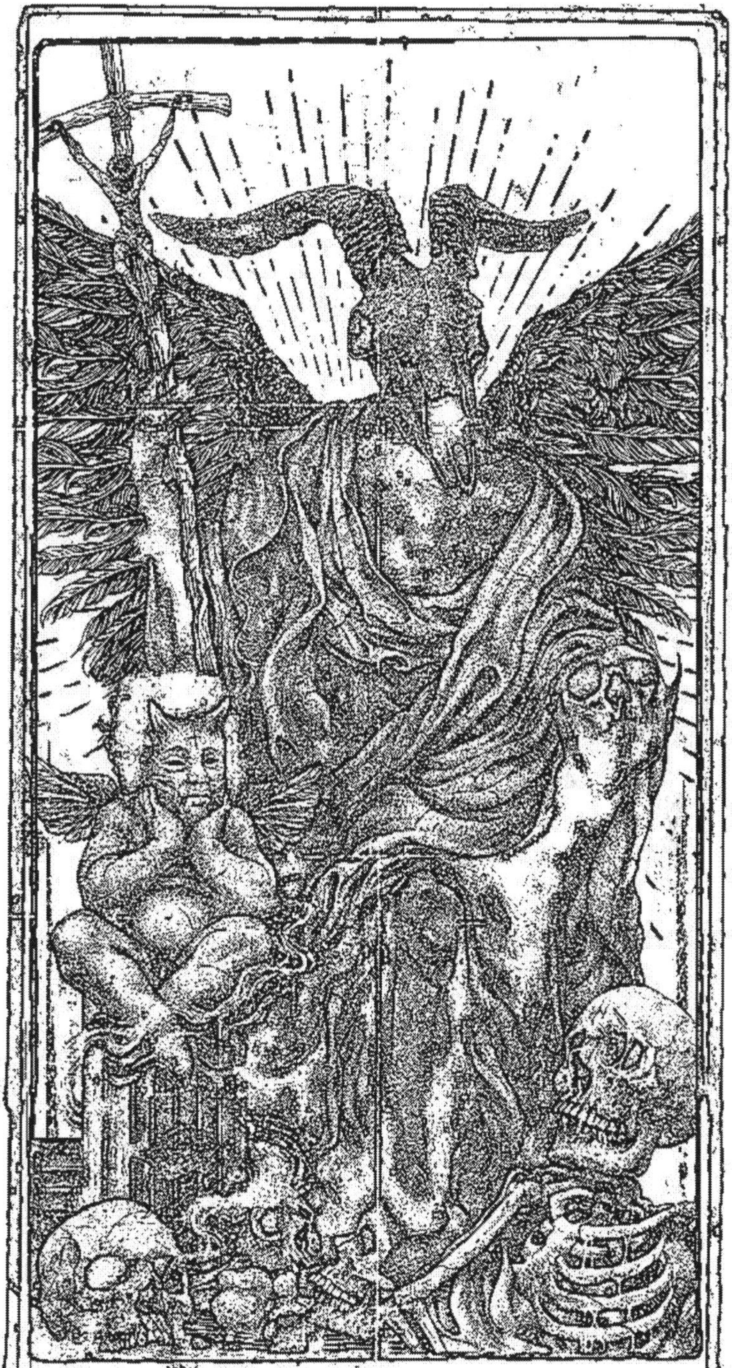

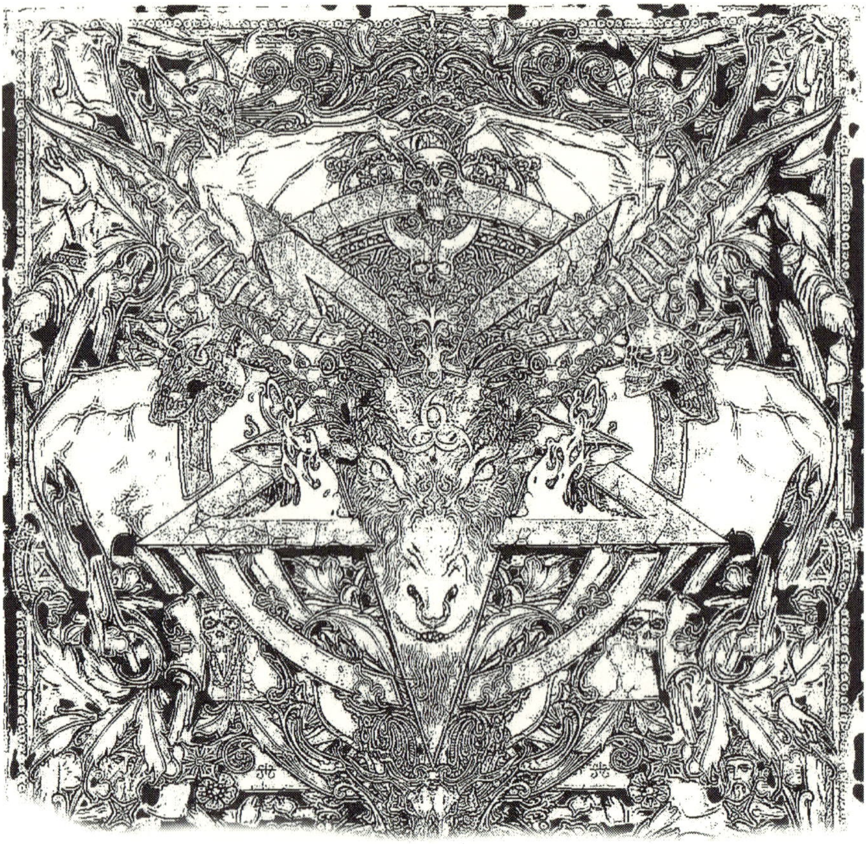

III

WAR

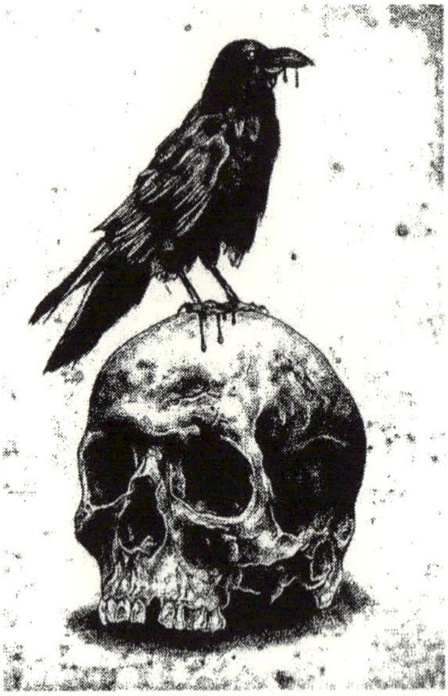

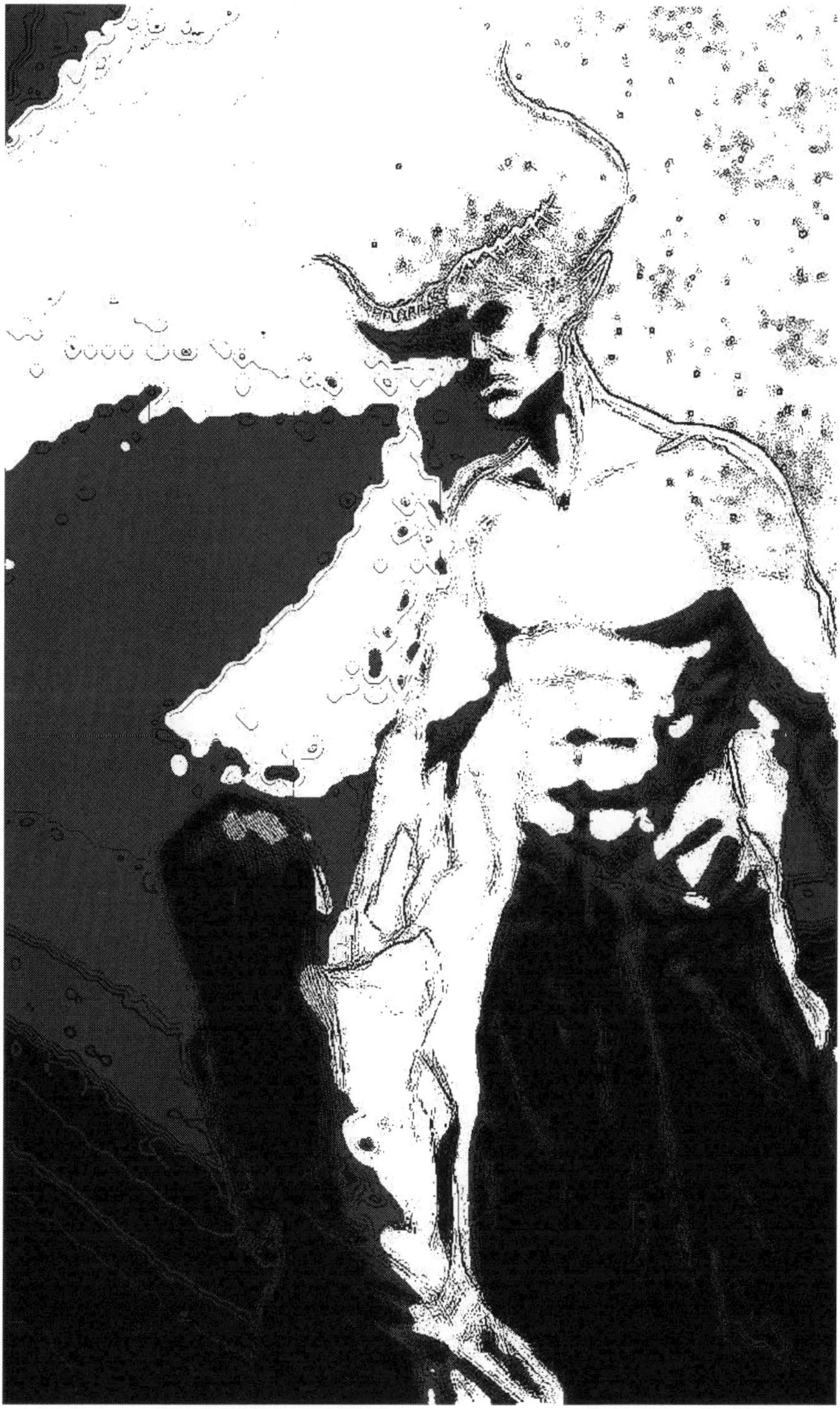

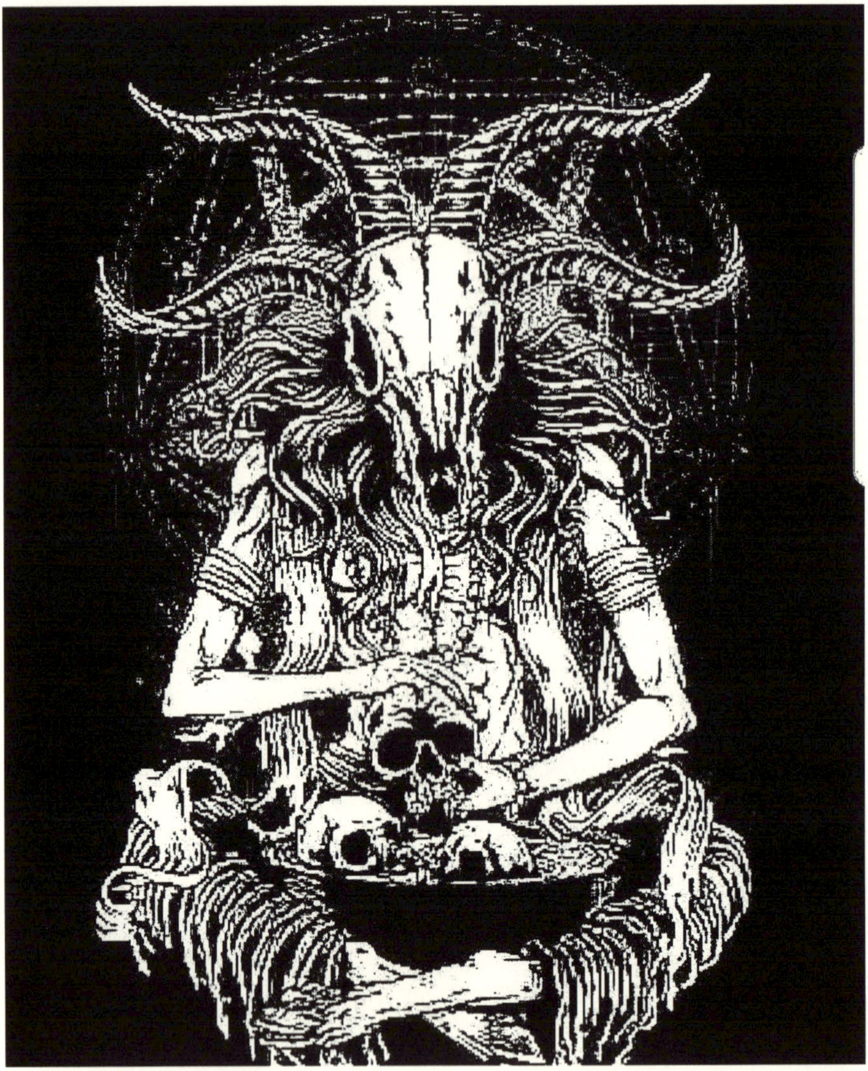

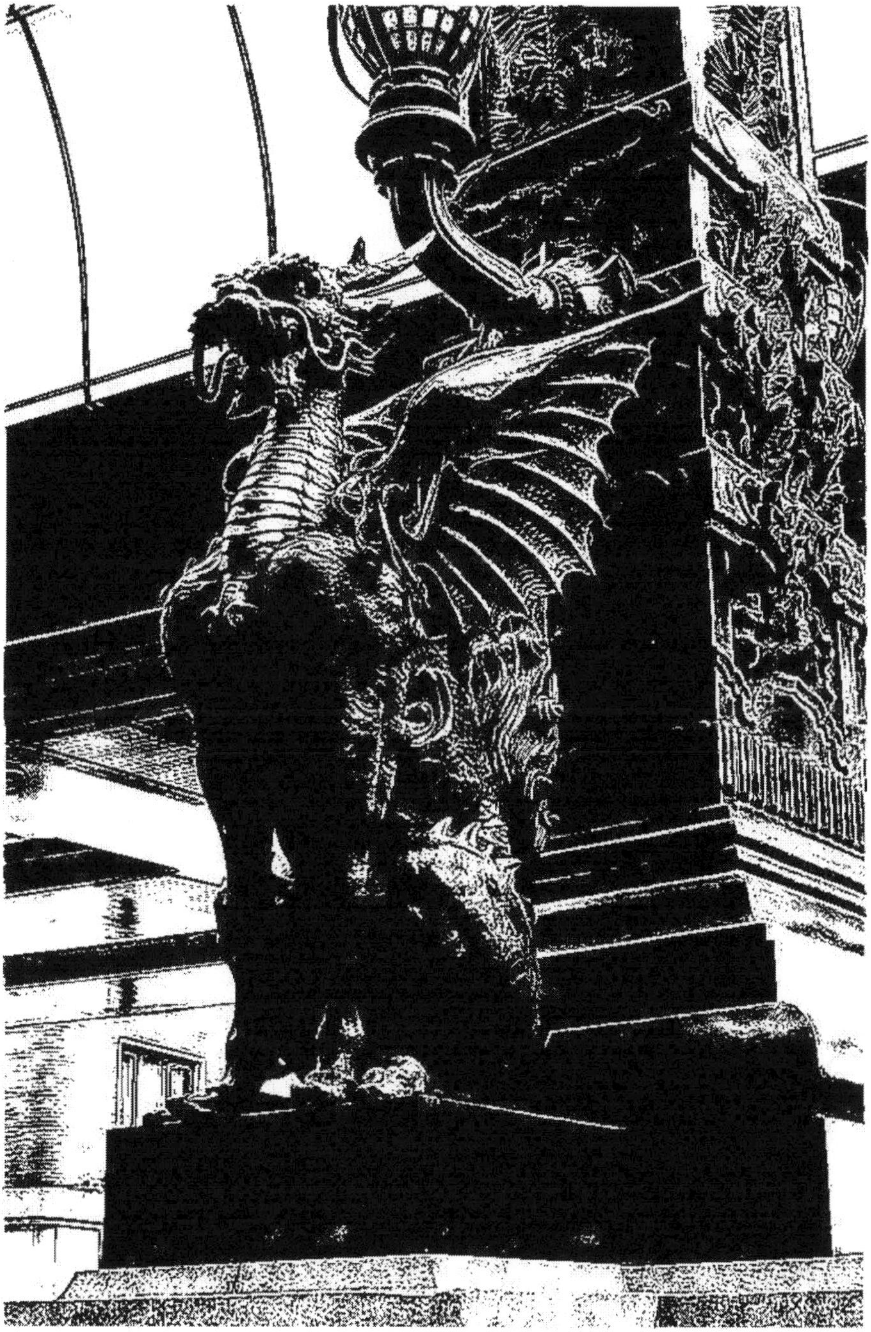

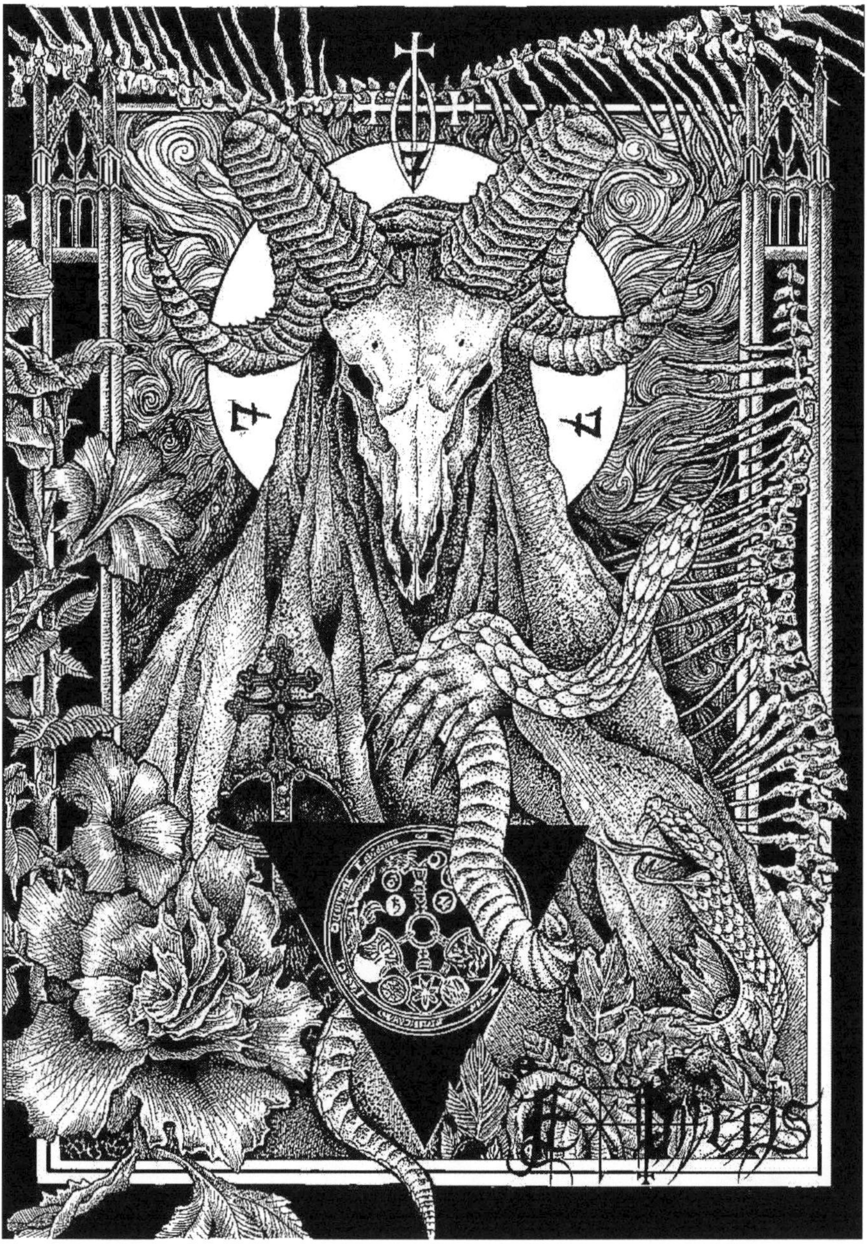

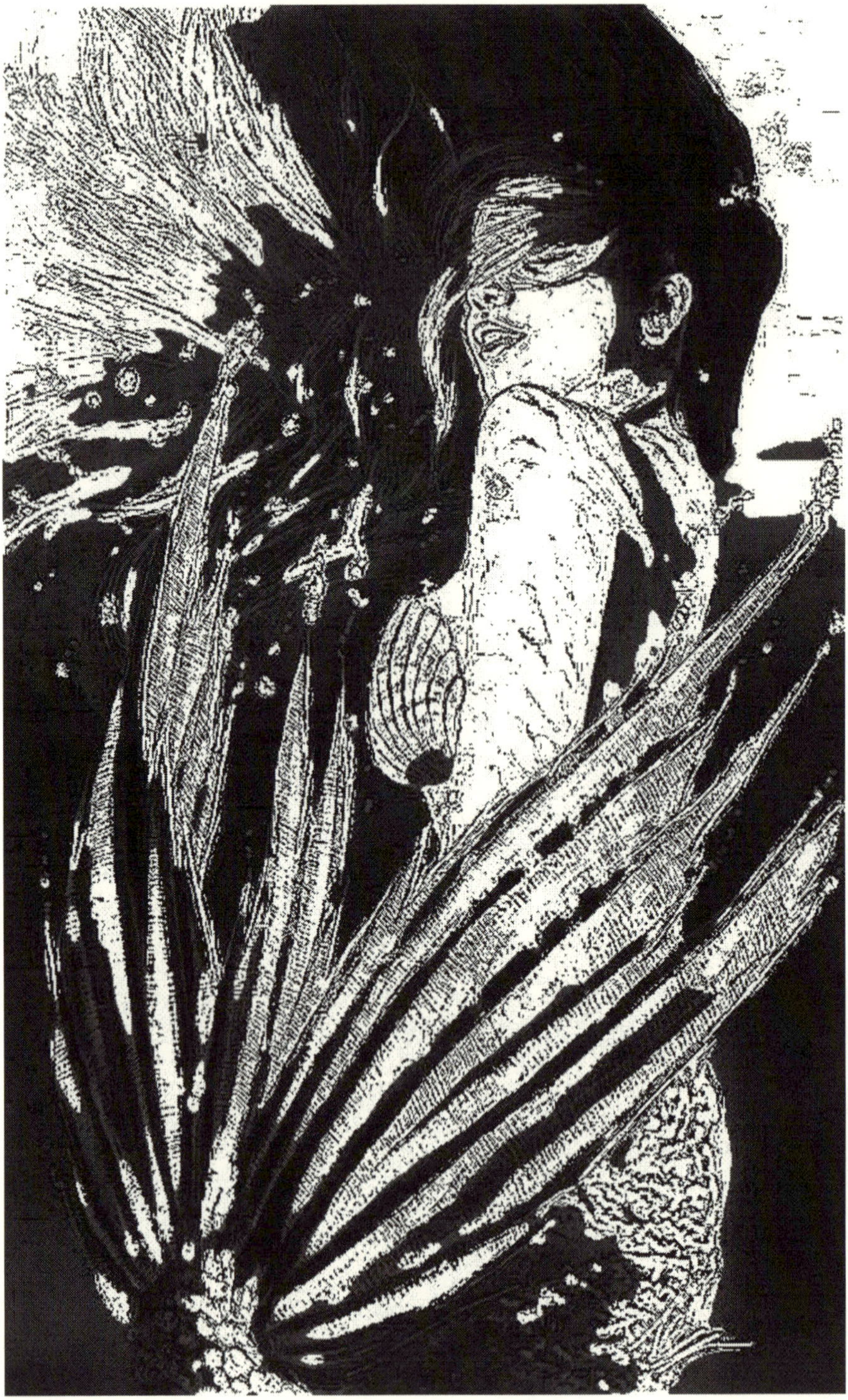

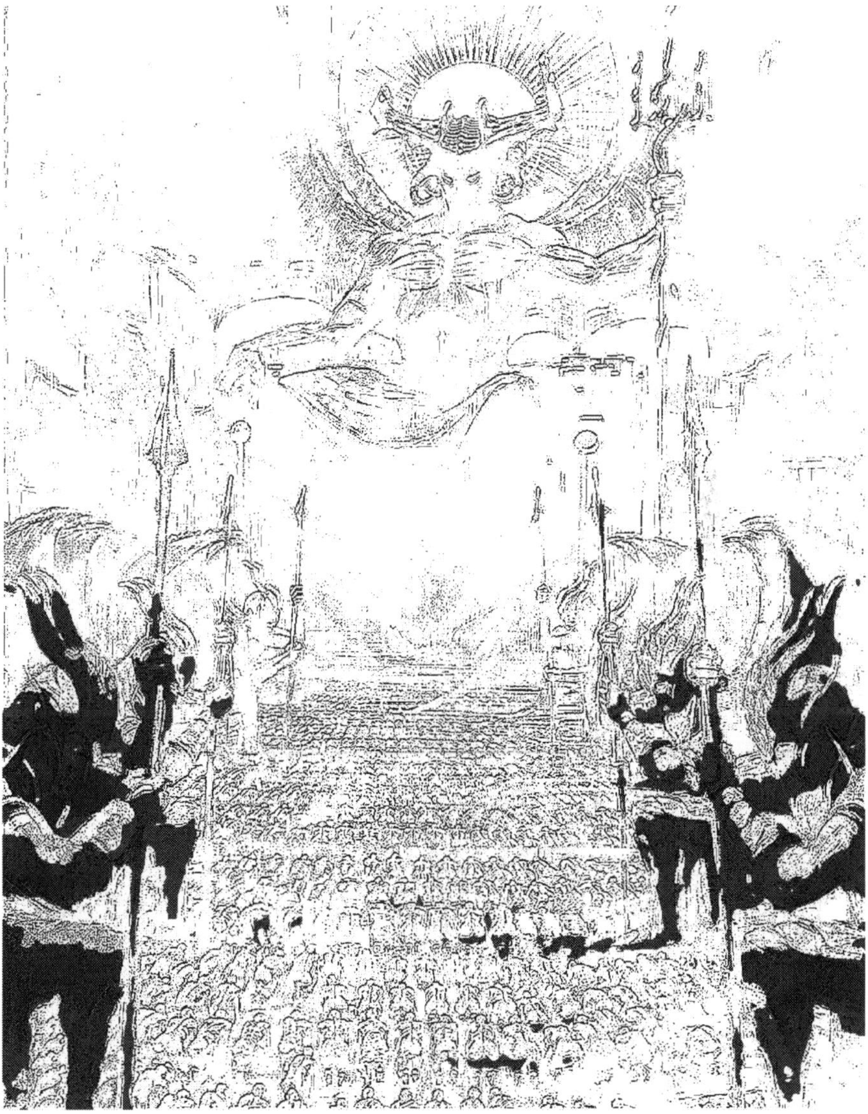

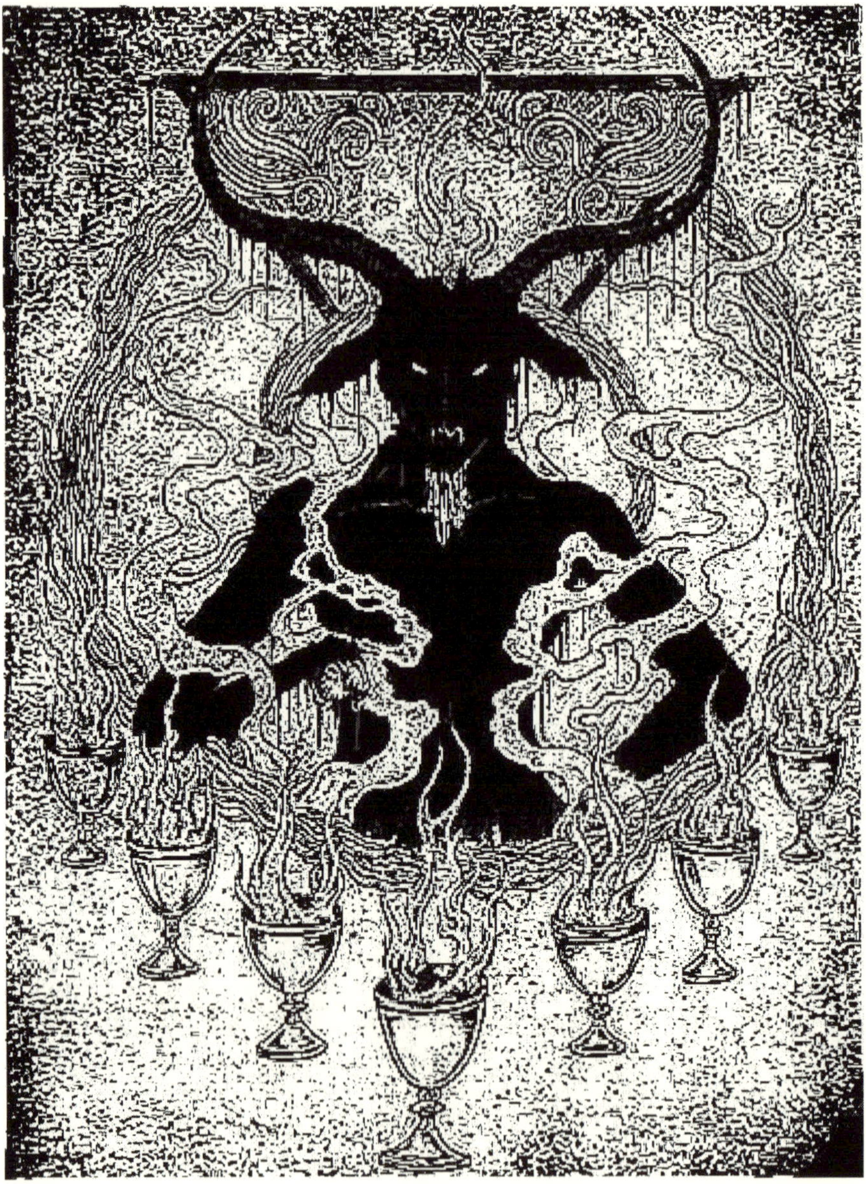

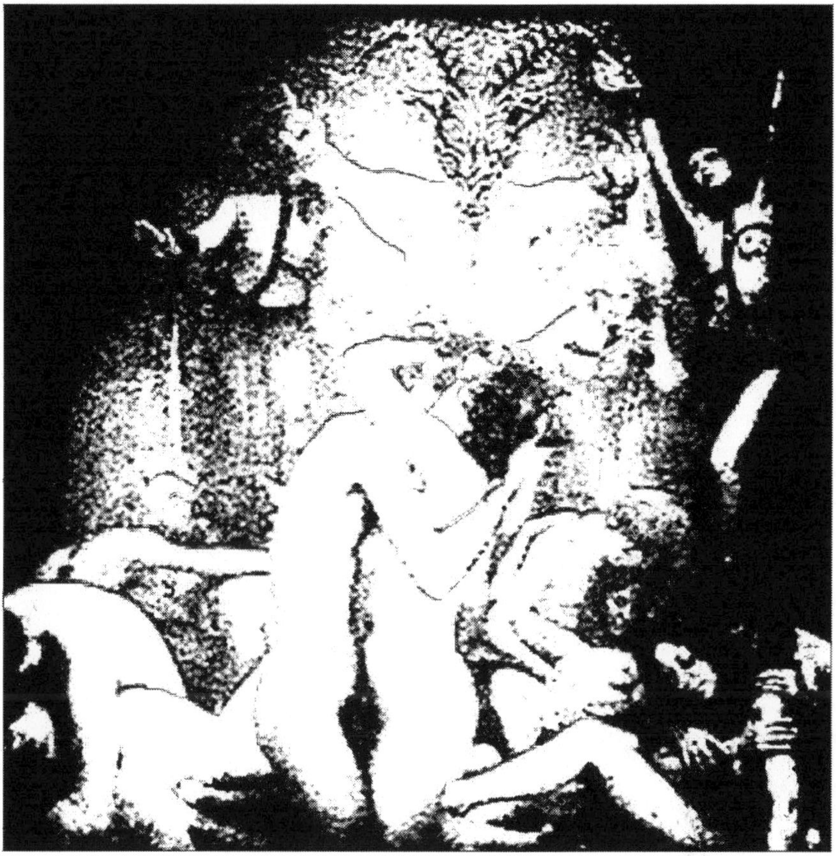

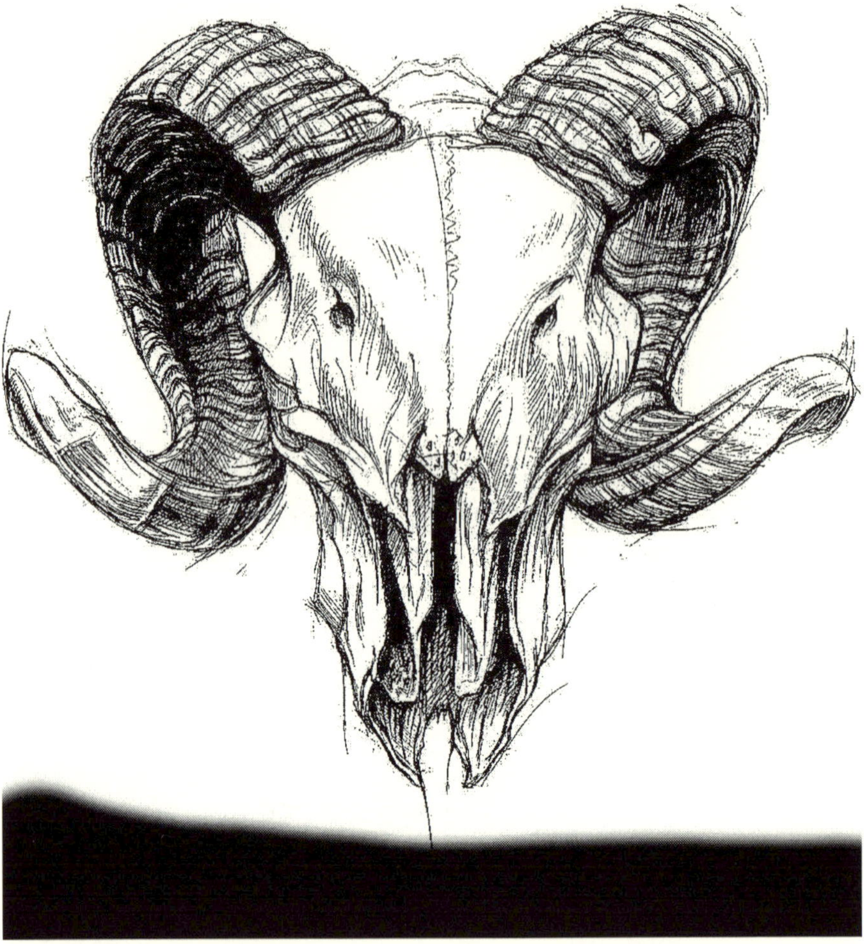

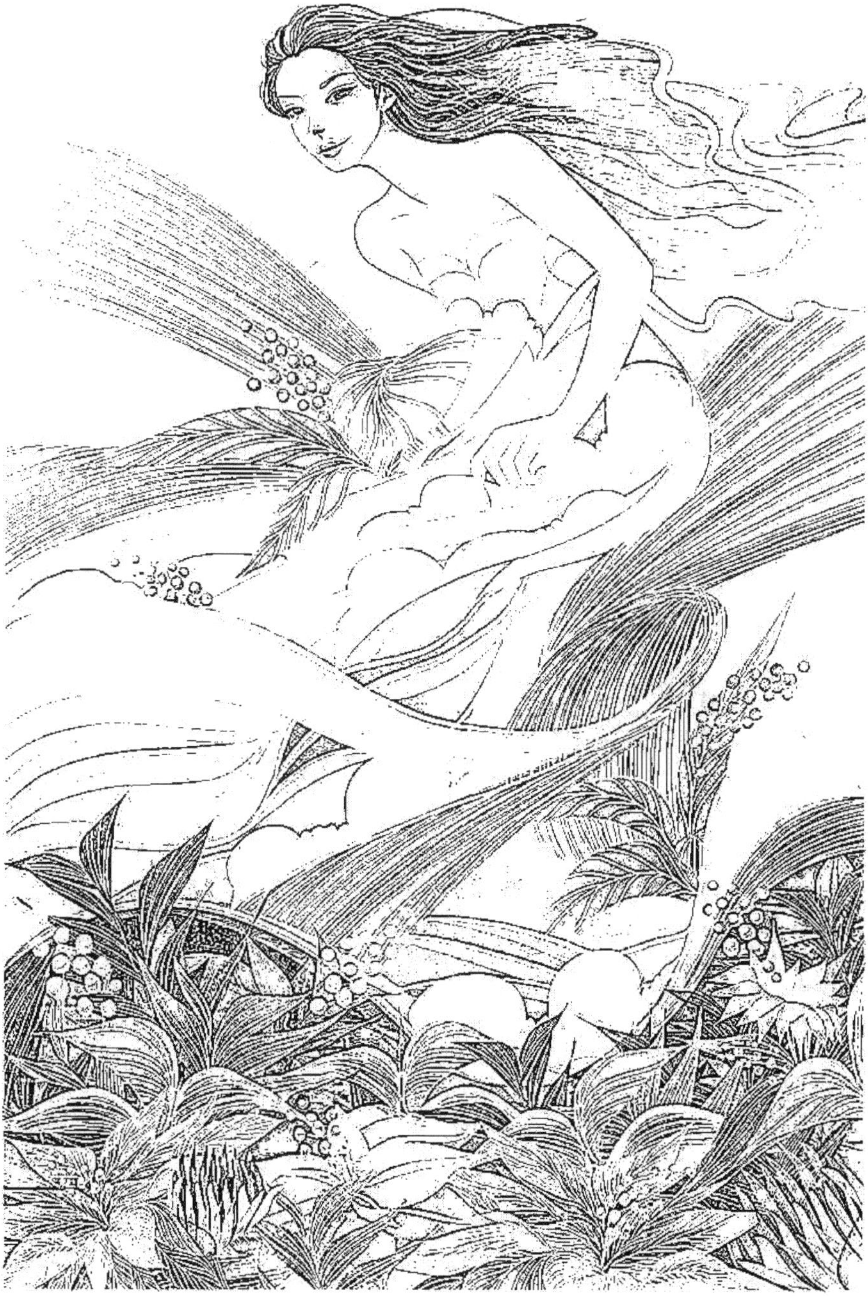

"He usually attended in the form of a monstrous goat"

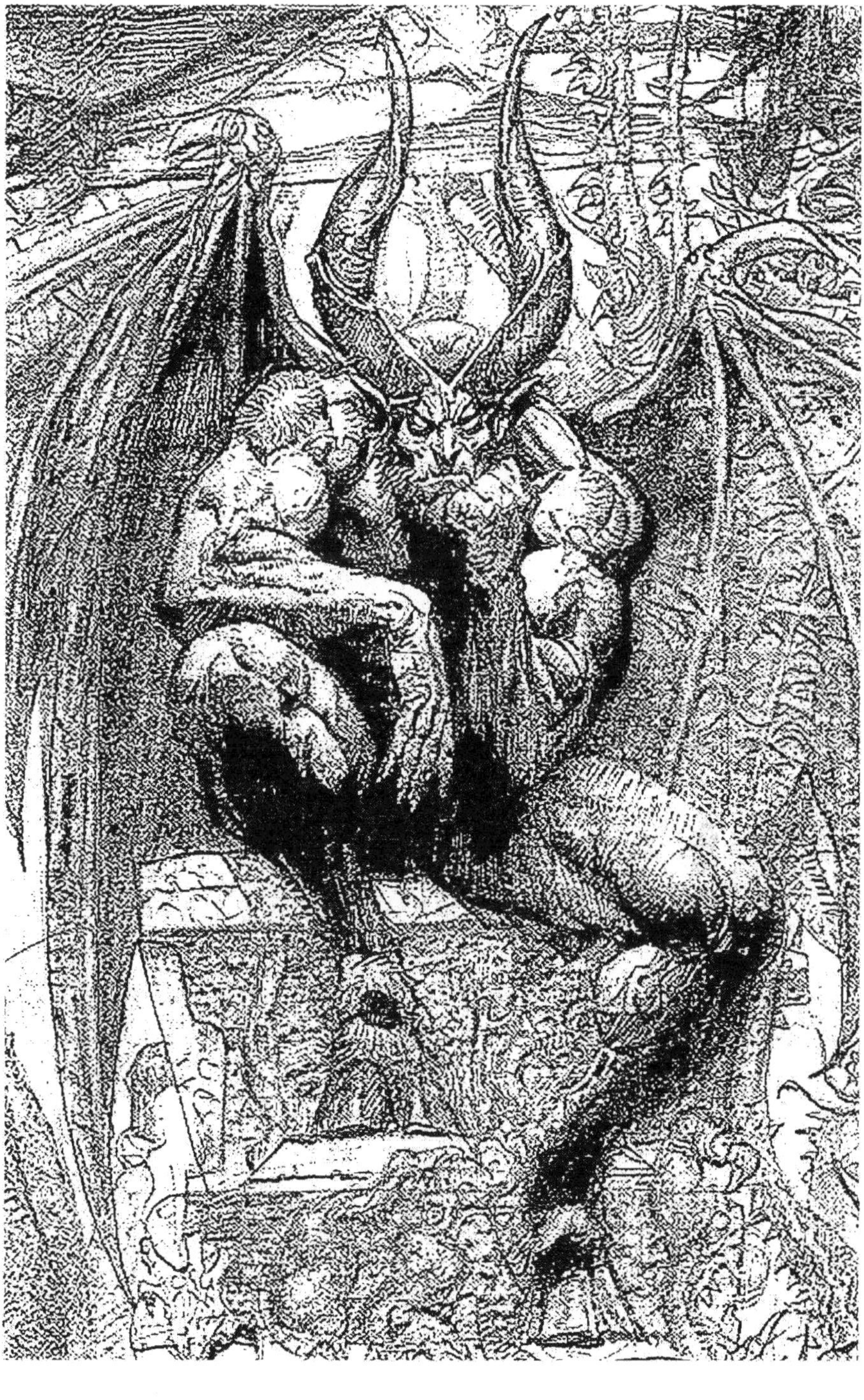

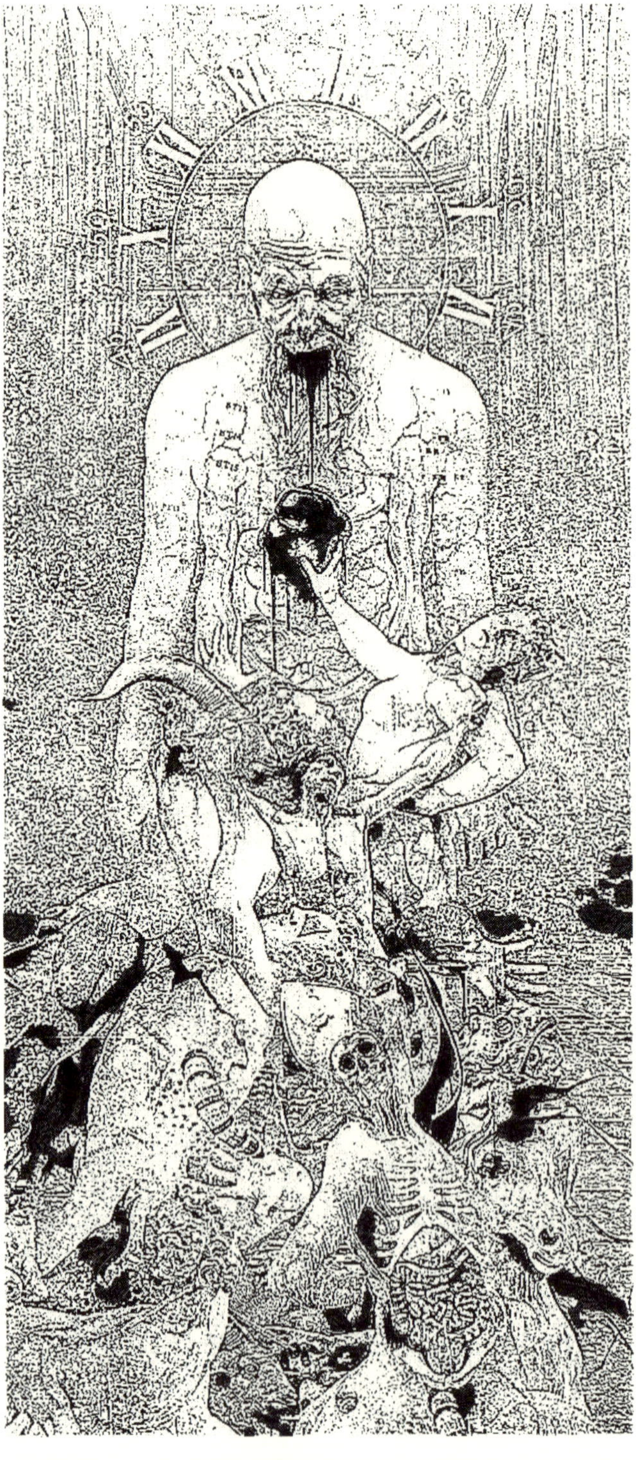

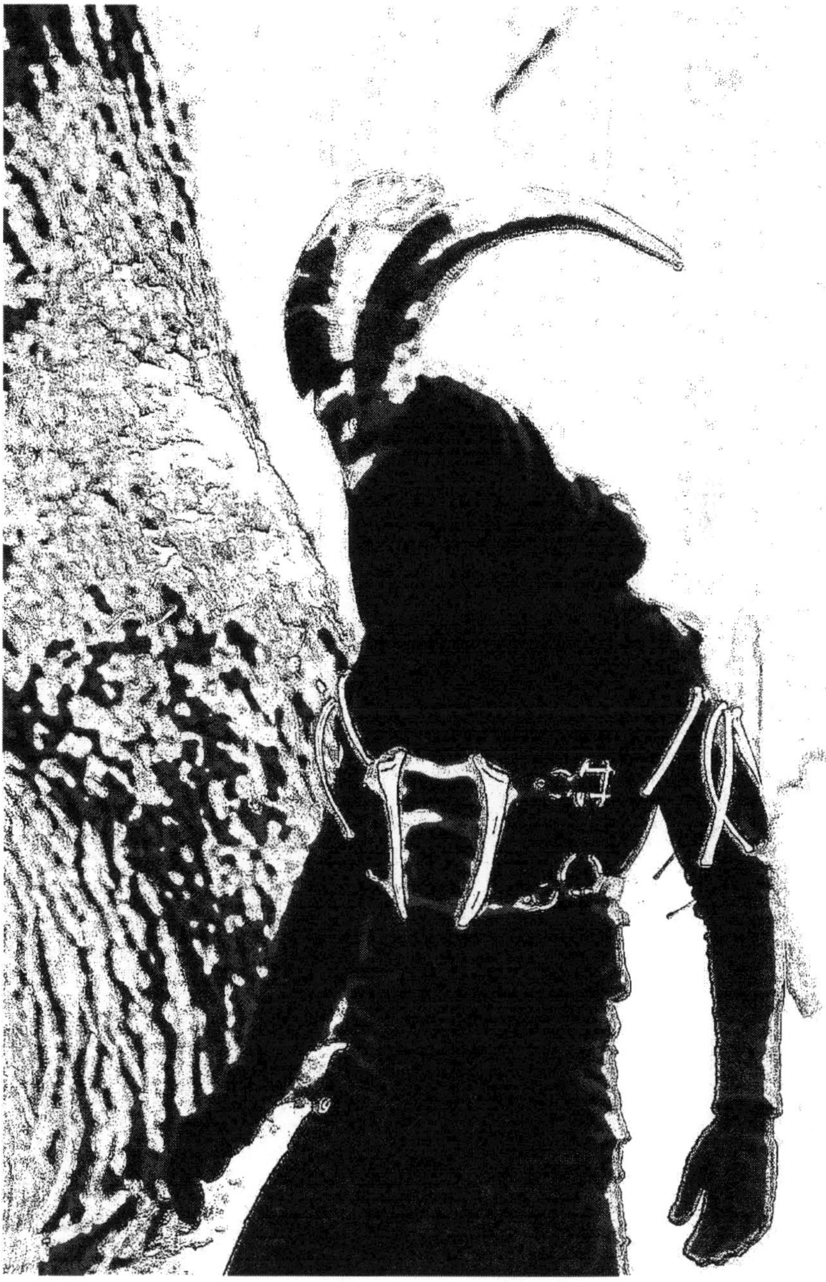

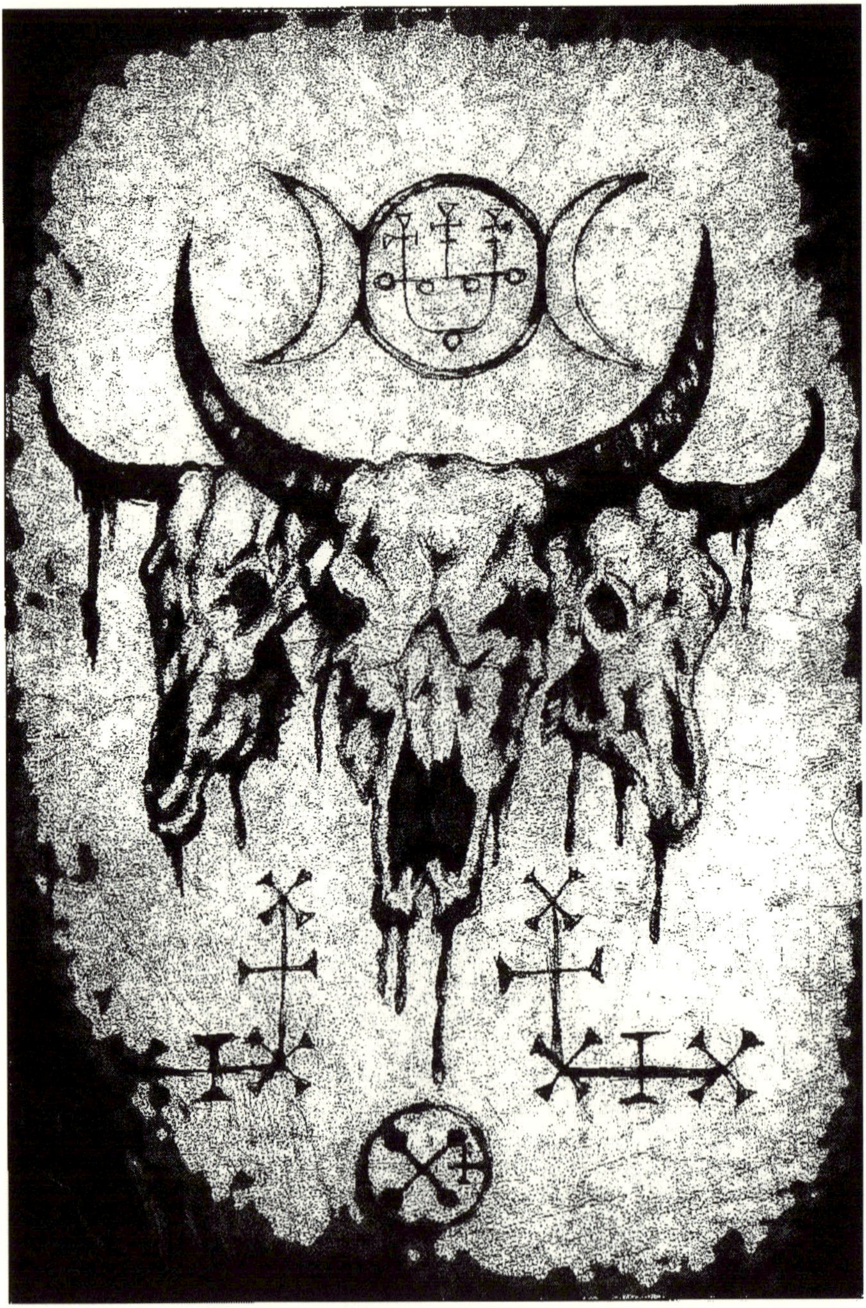

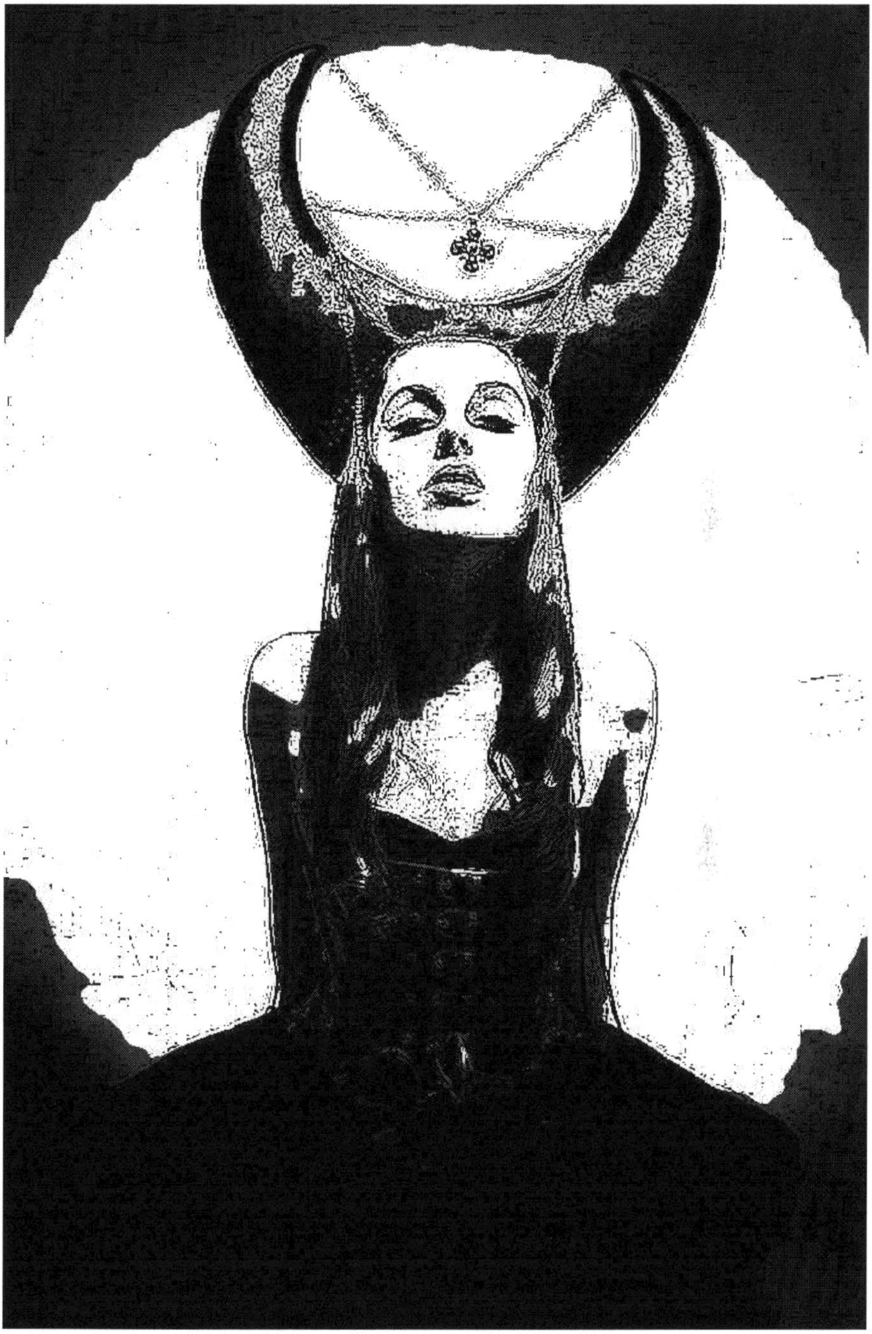

Made in the USA
Monee, IL
27 September 2021